ESSENTIALS FOR FURTHER ADVANCEMENT

(ENGLISH VERSION)

LI HONGZHI

ISBN: 1-58613-102-8

Second Translation Edition (February, 2000. USA)

Published by The Universe Publishing Company

Printed in the United States of America

Contents

Lunyu

"The Buddha Fa" is most profound; among all the theories in the world, it is the most intricate and extraordinary science. In order to explore this domain, humankind must fundamentally change its conventional thinking. Otherwise, the truth of the universe will forever remain a mystery to humankind, and everyday people will forever crawl within the boundary delimited by their own ignorance.

Then what exactly is "the Buddha Fa"? Is it a religion? Is it a philosophy? That is only the understanding of the "modernized Buddhist scholars," who merely study theories. They regard it as a philosophical category for critical studies and so-called research. Actually, "the Buddha Fa" is not only the tiny portion documented in the scriptures, for that is simply "the Buddha Fa" at an elementary level. "The Buddha Fa" is an insight into all mysteries. It encompasses everything and leaves out nothing—from particles and molecules to the universe, from the even smaller to the even greater. It is an exposition of the characteristic of the universe, "*Zhen-Shan-Ren*," expressed at different levels with different layers of meaning. It is also what the Tao School calls the "Tao," or what the Buddha School calls the "*Fa*."

As advanced as the present human science has become, it is still only part of the mysteries of the universe. Whenever we mention specific phenomena of "the Buddha Fa," someone will claim: "This is already the electronic age, and science is very advanced. Spaceships have already flown to other planets, yet you still bring up these outdated superstitions." To put it frankly, no matter how advanced a computer is, it is still no match for the human brain, which to this day remains an unfathomable enigma. However far a spaceship may fly, it cannot travel beyond this physical dimension in which our human race exists. What can be understood with modern human knowledge is extremely shallow and tiny; it is far from truly coming to terms with the truth of the universe. Some people even dare not face, touch upon, or admit the facts of phenomena that objectively exist, because they are too conservative and unwilling to change their conventional thinking. Only through "the Buddha Fa," can the mysteries of the universe, time-space, and the human body be completely unveiled. It is able to truly distinguish what is righteous from evil, good from bad, and eliminate all misconceptions while providing what is correct.

The guiding ideology for today's human science is confined only to this physical world in its research and development, as a subject will not be studied until it is recognized—it follows such a path. As for phenomena that are intangible and invisible in our dimension, but objectively exist and are reflected into our physical dimension as concrete manifestations, people dare not approach them, dismissing them as unknown phenomena. Opinionated people groundlessly try to reason that they are natural phenomena, while those with ulterior motives, against their own conscience, simply label all of them as superstition. Those who are indifferent simply stay away from the issue with the excuse that science is not yet advanced enough. If human beings are able to take a fresh look at themselves as well as the universe and change their rigid mentalities, humankind will make a leap forward. "The Buddha Fa" enables humankind to understand the immeasurable and boundless world. Throughout the ages, only "the Buddha Fa" has been able to perfectly provide a clear exposition of humanity, every dimension of material existence, life, and the entire universe.

Li Hongzhi
June 2, 1992

Wealth with Virtue

The ancients said, "Money is something external to this

3

physical body." Everyone knows it, yet everyone pursues it. A young man seeks it to satisfy his desires; a young woman wants it for glamour and luxury; an elderly person goes after it to take care of himself in his old age; a learned person desires it for fame; a public official fulfills his duty for it, etc. Hence, everybody pursues it.

Some people even compete and fight for it; those who are aggressive take risks for it; hot-tempered people resort to violence for it; a jealous person might die for it in anger. It is the duty of the ruler and officials to bring wealth to the populace, yet promotion of money-worship is the worst policy one could adopt. Wealth without virtue will harm all sentient beings, while wealth with virtue is what all people hope for. Therefore, one cannot be affluent without promoting virtue.

Virtue is accrued from past lives. Becoming a king, an official, wealthy, or nobility all come from virtue. No virtue, no gain; the loss of virtue denotes the loss of everything. Thus, those who seek power and wealth must first accumulate virtue; by suffering hardships and doing good deeds, one can collect virtue among the masses. To achieve this, one must understand the principle of cause and effect. Knowing this can enable officials and the populace to exercise self-restraint, and prosperity and peace will thereby prevail under heaven.

Li Hongzhi
January 27, 1995

Broad and Profound

The Fa and principles of Falun Dafa can provide guidance for anyone's cultivation practice, including for one's religious belief. This is the principle of the universe, the genuine Fa that has never been taught. People in the past were not allowed to know this principle of the universe (the Buddha Fa). It transcends all academic theories and moral principles of human society from ancient times to this day. What was taught by religions and what people experienced in the past were only superficialities and shallow phenomena. Its broad and profound inner meaning can only manifest itself to, and be experienced and understood by, practitioners at different levels of genuine cultivation. Only then can one truly see what the Fa is.

Li Hongzhi
February 6, 1995

Genuine Cultivation

My disciples of genuine cultivation, what I have taught
you is the Fa for cultivation of Buddha and Tao.
Nonetheless, you pour out your grievances to me over
the loss of your worldly interests, rather than feeling
upset for being unable to abandon everyday people's
attachments. Is this cultivation? Whether you can
abandon the everyday person's mindset is a fatal test
on your way to becoming a truly extraordinary being.
Every disciple of genuine cultivation must pass it, for it
is the dividing line between a practitioner and an
everyday person.

As a matter of fact, when you panic over infringements
upon your reputation, self-interests, and feelings among
everyday people, it already indicates that you cannot
relinquish everyday people's attachments. You must
remember this: Cultivation itself is not painful—the key
lies in your inability to release everyday people's
attachments. Only when you are about to let go of your
reputation, interests, and feelings will you feel pain.

You fell here from a holy, pure, and incomparably
splendid world because you had developed attachments
at that level. After falling into a world that is, in
comparison, most filthy, instead of cultivating yourself

6

to go back in a hurry, you do not let go of those filthy things that you cling to in this filthy world, and you are even quite panicked over a little bit of loss. Do you know that in order to save you the Buddha once begged for food among everyday people? Today, I once again make the door wide open and teach this Dafa to save you. I have never felt bitter for the numerous hardships I have suffered. Then what do you have that still cannot be relinquished? Can you bring to a heaven the things in your heart that you cannot give up?

Li Hongzhi
May 22, 1995

Be Clear Minded

I have told some practitioners that extreme thoughts are caused by thought-karma, but many practitioners now consider all their bad thoughts in everyday life to be thought-karma. This is incorrect. What is there for you to cultivate if you no longer have any bad thoughts?! If you are so pure, aren't you already a Buddha? This is a wrong understanding. Only when your mind violently reflects filthy thoughts, or curses Teacher, Dafa, other people, etc., and you cannot get rid of them or suppress them, would this be thought-karma. But there is also some weak thought-karma, though it is different from regular thoughts or ideas. You must be clear about this.

Li Hongzhi
May 23, 1995

Enlightenment

In the muddy human world, pearls and fish eyes are jumbled together. A Tathagata must descend to the world quietly. When he teaches the Fa, evil schools are bound to interfere. The Tao and the demonic ways are taught at the same time and in the same world. Amidst truth and falsehood, enlightening is important. How to distinguish them? There are bound to be exceptional people. Those who really have predestined relationships and can be enlightened will come one after another, entering the Tao and obtaining the Fa. They will distinguish the righteous from the evil, receive the genuine teachings, lighten their bodies, enhance their wisdom, strengthen their hearts, and board the boat of the Fa, sailing smoothly. How wonderful! Strive forward with every effort until the completion of cultivation.

Those who survive the world without direction and with poor enlightenment quality live for money and die for power, being joyful or anxious over petty gains. They compete bitterly against each other, thus accruing karma throughout their lives. When such people hear the Fa, they laugh at it and spit from their mouths the word "superstition," as they are bound to find it hard to understand and hard to believe in their hearts. Such people are the low-level persons who are difficult to save. Their karma is so much that it has enveloped their bodies and sealed off their wisdom; their original nature is gone.

Li Hongzhi
June 14, 1995

Why One Cannot See

Seeing is believing, and what is not seen is disbelieved. This is the view of a low-level person. Humans are in delusion and have created a lot of karma, thereby obscuring their original nature: So how could they see? Enlightening comes before seeing. Cultivate your heart and eliminate your karma. Once your original nature comes forth you will be able to see. Yet, with or without seeing, an exceptional person can depend on his enlightening to complete cultivation. As to most people, they may or may not see, and this is determined by their levels or their inborn quality. A practitioner usually does not see because he is in pursuit of seeing—this is an attachment. Thus, until it is given up he will not see. This is mostly due to the obstacles from karma, an unsuitable environment, or one's cultivation way. There are a multitude of reasons, varying from person to person. Even a person who is able to see may not see clearly, for only seeing unclearly can one enlighten to the Tao. When a person can see everything clearly as if he were personally on the scene, he has achieved *kaigong* and cannot practice cultivation any further since there is nothing for him to enlighten to.

Li Hongzhi
June 16, 1995

Learning the Fa

In learning Dafa, intellectuals should be aware of a most prominent problem: namely, they study Dafa in the same way everyday people study theoretical writings,[1] such as selecting relevant quotations from renowned people to examine their own conduct. This will hinder a practitioner's progress. Furthermore, upon learning that

---

[1] "theoretical writings"—this is referring to the theories of Marxism, Leninism, Maoism, etc.

Dafa has profound, inner meaning and high-level things that can guide cultivation practice at different levels, some people even attempt to examine it word by word, but find nothing in the end. These habits, acquired from studying political theories over a long period of time, are also factors that interfere with cultivation practice; they lead to a misunderstanding of the Fa.

While learning the Fa, you should not search for relevant parts, stubbornly intending to solve a particular problem. In fact, this (excluding those problems needing immediate solutions) is also a form of attachment. The only way to gain a good understanding of Dafa is to study it without any intention. Each time you finish reading <u>Zhuan Falun</u>, you have made progress so long as you have gained some understanding. Even if you understood only one point after reading it, you have truly made progress.

Actually, in cultivation practice you ascend by improving yourself gradually and unknowingly. Keep in mind: One should gain things naturally without pursuing them.

Li Hongzhi
September 9, 1995

How to Provide Assistance

Many assistants in different regions have a very high-level understanding of Dafa. They are able to set a good example with their conduct and do a good job organizing their practice groups. Yet there are also some assistants who have not done so well, and this mainly manifests in their methods of work. For instance, in order to make the practitioners listen to them and to make it easier to carry out their work, some assistants have done their work by issuing orders—this is not permitted. Learning the Fa should be voluntary. If a practitioner does not want to do so from the bottom of his heart, no problem can be solved. Instead, conflicts may arise. If this is not corrected, conflicts will intensify, thus severely undermining people's learning the Fa.

Even more serious, some assistants, in order to make practitioners believe and obey them, often circulate some hearsay or something sensational to increase their prestige, or they do unique things to show off. All of these are not allowed. Our assistants serve others on a voluntary basis; they are not the master, nor should they have such attachments.

Then how can we do the assistant job well? First off,

you should treat yourself as one of the practitioners instead of considering yourself someone above them. If there is something that you do not know in your work, you should humbly discuss it with others. If you have done something wrong, you should sincerely tell the practitioners, "I, too, am a practitioner just as you are, so it's inevitable that there be mistakes in my work. Now that I have made a mistake, let's do what is right." With the sincerity to have all practitioners collaborate to get things done, what results will you find? No one will say that you are good for nothing. Instead, they will think that you have learned the Fa well and are open-minded. In fact, with Dafa here, everyone is studying it. With every move an assistant makes, whether good or not, the practitioners will measure it with Dafa and see it clearly. Once you have the intention of building yourself up, the practitioners will think that you have a xinxing problem. Therefore, only by being modest can you do things well. Your prestige is established based upon a good understanding of the Fa. How can a practitioner be free of mistakes?

Li Hongzhi
September 10, 1995

Firmament

The vastness of the universe and the enormity of the celestial bodies can never be understood by man through exploration. The minuteness of matter can never be detected by man. The human body is so mysterious that it is beyond man's knowledge, which is merely a scratch on the surface. Life is so abundant and complex that it will forever remain an eternal enigma to mankind.

Li Hongzhi
September 24, 1995

Realms

A wicked person is born of jealousy. Out of selfishness and anger he complains about unfairness towards himself.

A benevolent person always has a heart of compassion. With no discontent or hatred, he takes hardship as joy.

An enlightened being has no attachments at all. He quietly observes the everyday people blinded by delusion.

14

Li Hongzhi
September 25, 1995

What is Emptiness?

What is emptiness? Being free of attachments is the true state of emptiness. It does not mean that there is no existence of matter. Zen Buddhism has reached the end of its Dharma, however, and has nothing to teach. In this chaotic Dharma-ending Period, some scholars still stubbornly hold on to its theory of emptiness, acting irrational and absurd, as though they are enlightened to the fundamentals of its philosophy. Its founder, Boddhidharma, himself acknowledged that his Dharma could only be effective for six generations, and after that there would be nothing to pass down. Why not awaken to it? If one says that everything is empty, with no Fa, no Buddha, no image, no self, and no existence, what thing is Boddhidharma? If there is no Dharma, what thing is Zen Buddhism's theory of emptiness? If there is no Buddha, no image, who is Sakyamuni? If there is no name, no image, no self, no existence, and everything is empty, why do you bother to eat and drink? Why do you wear clothes? What if your eyes were dug out? Why are you so attached to the seven emotions and six desires of an everyday person? Actually, what a

15

Tathagata means by "emptiness" is being free from all the attachments of an everyday person. Non-omission is the true essence of emptiness. To begin with, the universe exists because of matter and is composed of and remains as matter. How can it be empty? The Dharma that is not taught by a Tathagata is bound to be short-lived, and its principles will cease to exist. The Dharma of an Arhat is not the Buddha Fa. Enlighten to it! Enlighten to it!

Li Hongzhi
September 28, 1995

Determination

With Teacher here, you are full of confidence. Without Teacher here, you lose your interest in cultivation. It appears as though you cultivate yourself for Teacher and have come here out of short-lived interest. This is a major weakness of an average person. Sakyamuni, Jesus, Lao Zi, and Confucius have been gone for over two thousand years, yet their disciples have never felt that they cannot practice cultivation without their masters around. Cultivation is your own matter, and nobody else can do it for you. The teacher can only tell you the law and principles on the surface. It is your

16

own responsibility to cultivate your heart, give up your desires, attain wisdom, and eliminate confusion. If you have come here out of short-lived interest, your mind will certainly be undetermined. While living in human society, you are bound to forget the fundamentals. If you do not firmly hold to your faith, you will gain nothing in this life. It is not known when there will be another chance. It's very hard!

Li Hongzhi
October 6, 1995

The Teachings in Buddhism are the Weakest and Tiniest Portion of the Buddha Fa

All sentient beings! Never use Buddhism to measure the Dafa of Zhen-Shan-Ren, because it is immeasurable. People have already become accustomed to calling the scriptures of Buddhism the Fa. In fact, the cosmic bodies are so vast that they are beyond a Buddha's understanding of the universe. Taiji of the Tao School is also a low-level understanding of the universe. At the level of everyday people there is no actual Fa, except for a tiny smattering of phenomena on the boundary of the universe that have the capacity to enable one to practice cultivation. Since everyday people are beings

17

at the lowest level, they are not allowed to know the real Buddha Fa. But people have heard sages say: worshipping Buddha may plant the causal seeds for the opportunity to practice cultivation; cultivators who chant incantations can receive protection from higher beings; observing precepts can enable one to reach a cultivator's standard. Throughout history people have been studying: "Is what the Enlightened One taught the Buddha Fa?" The Tathagata's teaching is the manifestation of Buddha-nature, and it can also be called a manifestation of Fa. But it is not the universe's actual Fa, because in the past people were absolutely prohibited from knowing the Buddha Fa's true manifestation. The Buddha Fa could only be enlightened to by someone who had reached a high level through cultivation practice, so it was even more the case that people were not allowed to know the true essence of cultivation practice. Falun Dafa has for the first time throughout the ages left the characteristic of the universe (the Buddha Fa) to human beings; this amounts to leaving them a ladder to ascend to heaven. So how can you measure the Dafa of the universe with what was once taught in Buddhism?

Li Hongzhi
October 8, 1995

What is Wisdom?

People think that the renowned persons, scholars and different sorts of experts in human society are quite great. In fact, they are all very insignificant, for they are everyday people. Their knowledge is only that tiny bit understood by the modern science of human society. In the vast universe, from the most macroscopic to the most microscopic, human society is exactly in the very middle, in the most outer layer, and on the most outer surface. Also, its living beings are the lowest form of existence, so their understanding of matter and mind is very limited, superficial, and pitiful. Even with all of mankind's knowledge grasped, one would remain an everyday person.

Li Hongzhi
October 9, 1995

It is not a Job, but Cultivation Practice

Whether you can follow the requirements I have set for assistance centers is a very important matter of principle, for at stake is the way the Fa is spread in the future. Why can't you give up the habits you have developed over a long period of time in bureaucratic offices? Do not treat assistance centers as administrative offices in human society and adopt their methods and approaches, such as issuing documents, launching policy implementations, or improving some type of understanding. A cultivator of Dafa should only upgrade his xinxing and improve his Fruit Status and level in his cultivation practice. Sometimes even a meeting is held in the format of the everyday people's workplace. For example, some kind of official will make a speech, and a certain leader will give a summary. Now, even the state is trying to reform those corrupted practices and bureaucratic procedures in society. As a practitioner, you have already known that every aspect of mankind is no longer good in the Dharma-ending Period. Why can't you give up the work methods that are most unsuitable for cultivation practice? We absolutely will never turn it into an administrative institution or an enterprise in society.

Before, some retired people with nothing to do found Falun Dafa good and offered help so as to fill an aching void in their leisurely lives. Of course this won't do! Falun Dafa is for cultivation practice, and it is not a job. All of our personnel must first be genuine practitioners with high-level xinxing, and they are role models for xinxing cultivation. We do not need the types of leaders like those among everyday people.

Li Hongzhi
October 12, 1995

Practicing Cultivation After Retirement

It is a great pity that some practitioners who attended my lectures and have good inborn quality have stopped practicing because they are busy with work. If they were average, everyday people, I would say nothing more and leave them alone. But these people still have some promise. The human morality is declining a thousand miles a day, and everyday people are all drifting along with the current. The farther away from the Tao, the more difficult to return through cultivation. As a matter of fact, cultivation practice is about cultivating one's heart. In particular, the complex environment of the workplace provides a good opportunity for you to upgrade your xinxing. Once retired, won't you lose the best environment for your cultivation practice? What will you cultivate without any conflicts? How can you improve yourself? One's life is limited. Oftentimes you plan things quite well, but do you know whether you will have sufficient time left for your cultivation? Cultivation practice is not child's play, and it is more

21

serious than anything of everyday people; it is not something to take for granted. Once you miss the opportunity, when will you be able to get a human body again in the six paths of reincarnation? Opportunity knocks but once. Once the illusion that you cannot relinquish disappears, you will realize what you have lost.

Li Hongzhi
October 13, 1995

When the Fa is Right

When man does not have virtue, natural calamities and man-made disasters will abound. When the earth does not have virtue, everything will wither and fall. When heaven deviates from the Tao, the ground will crack, the sky will collapse, and all the cosmos will be empty. When the Fa is right, the universe will be right. Life will flourish, heaven and earth will be stable, and the Fa will exist forever.

Li Hongzhi
November 12, 1995

Sage

He is on a Providential mission in this world as well as in heaven above. With mighty virtue and a benevolent heart, he brings forth lofty ideals while minding minor details. With broad knowledge of the law and principles, he is able to unravel uncertainties. By benefiting society and saving people, he builds up his merit naturally.

Li Hongzhi
November 17, 1995

Seeking Discipleship with Teacher

Dafa is being spread far and wide. Those who hear about it are looking for it. Those who have obtained it are delighted with it. The number of cultivators is increasing daily and becoming innumerable. Nonetheless, most of the self-learners have the intention of formally seeking discipleship with Teacher, for they are concerned that they might not have received the genuine teachings if they have not seen Teacher in person. This is actually due to a lack of deep understanding of the Fa. My teaching Dafa widely is to offer salvation to all. Whoever learns it is my disciple. Without following old rituals and conventions, I ignore superficial formalities and only look at one's heart. If you do not genuinely cultivate yourself, what's the use of formally acknowledging me as "Teacher?" A genuine practitioner will gain things naturally without pursuing them. All the *gong* and the Fa lie in the books, and one will naturally obtain them by reading Dafa. Those who learn it will change automatically, and they will already be in the Tao by reading the books over and over again. Teacher will certainly have *fashen* protecting them quietly. With perseverance, they are bound to attain the Right Fruit in the future.

Li Hongzhi
December 8, 1995

An Explicit Reminder

At present there is a very prominent problem: namely, when some practitioners' *yuanshen* leave their bodies, they see or come into contact with certain dimensions at certain levels. Feeling it is so wonderful and that everything there is of genuine existence, they do not want to return. This has resulted in the death of their physical bodies. So they stayed in that realm and could not come back. Yet none of them had reached beyond the Three Realms. I have spoken of this issue before.

Do not get attached to any dimension in your cultivation. Only when you have completed the entire course of cultivation can you achieve completion. So when your yuanshen goes out, no matter how wonderful you find those places, you must return.

We also have some practitioners who have a misunderstanding. They think that once they practice Falun Dafa they are assured that their physical bodies will never die. Our cultivation system does cultivate both mind and body. While he practices cultivation, a practitioner can prolong his life. But some people have not diligently made progress in their Shi-Jian-Fa cultivation and they always linger at a certain level. After much effort to move up to another level, they then linger at that level again. Cultivation practice is a serious matter, so it is difficult to guarantee that one's life will not come to an end at the predestined time. This problem, however, does not exist for cultivation practice beyond Shi-Jian-Fa. But the situation within Shi-Jian-Fa is more complicated.

Li Hongzhi
December 21, 1995

For Whom do You Practice Cultivation?

When some people resort to the media to criticize qigong, some practitioners waver in determination and give up their practice; it is as though those who take advantage of the media are wiser than the Buddha Fa, and that some practitioners practice cultivation for others. There are also people who become scared in the face of pressure and give up their cultivation. Can these kinds of people achieve the Right Fruit? At the crucial moment, won't they even betray Buddha? Isn't fear an attachment? Cultivation practice is like great waves washing away the sand: what remains is gold.

As a matter of fact, from ancient times to the present, human society has had a principle called inter-generation and inter-inhibition. So where there is good, there is bad; where there is right, there is evil; where there is compassion, there is wickedness; where there are humans, there are ghosts; where there are Buddhas, there are demons. It is even more present in human society. Where there is positive, there is negative; where there is advocacy, there is opposition; where there are those who believe, there are those who disbelieve; where there are good people, there are bad ones; where there are selfless people, there are selfish ones; and where there are people who can make sacrifices for others, there are people who will stop at nothing to benefit themselves. This was a principle in the past. Therefore, if an individual, a group, or even a nation wants to accomplish something good, there will be an equal amount of negative resistance. After success, one will thus feel that it was hard won and should be treasured. This was how mankind developed in the past (the principle of inter-generation and inter-inhibition will change in the future).

Speaking from another perspective, cultivation practice is supernormal. No matter who a person is, isn't his criticism of qigong from an everyday person's view? Does he have any right to deny the Buddha Fa and cultivation? Can any of mankind's organizations rise above Gods and Buddhas? Do those who criticize qigong have the capacity to command Buddhas? Will Buddhas be bad simply because he says so? Will Buddhas cease to exist simply because he claims that there are no Buddhas? The Dharma's tribulation during the "Great Cultural Revolution" resulted from the evolution of cosmic phenomena. Buddhas, Taos and Gods all follow heaven's will. The Dharma's tribulation was a tribulation for humans and religions, rather than a tribulation for Buddhas.

The greatest reason for religions being undermined is

the degeneration of the human mind. People worship Buddha not to cultivate Buddhahood, but to seek Buddha's blessings so that they can make a fortune, eliminate adversities, have a son, or lead a comfortable life. Everyone accrued a lot of karma in previous lives. How could one live comfortably? How could a person not pay for his karma after doing bad deeds? Seeing the human mind not right, demons have come out of their caves one after another to bring trouble and chaos to the human world. Upon seeing the human mind not right, Gods and Buddhas left their posts and abandoned the temples one after another. Many foxes, weasels, ghosts, and snakes have been brought into the temples by those who come to pray for wealth and profit. How can such temples not be in trouble? Human beings are the sinners. Buddhas do not punish people, because all people are driven by ignorance and have already done harm to themselves. Moreover, they have accrued great amounts of karma for themselves, and soon a great catastrophe will await them. Would there still be any need to punish them? In fact, if one does something wrong, one is bound to suffer retribution sometime in the future. It is just that people do not realize or believe it; they regard mishaps as accidents.

Regardless of whether it is a person or a social force that tells you not to practice cultivation anymore, you then give up your cultivation. Do you practice cultivation for them? Will they give you the Right Fruit? Isn't your inclination toward them a blind faith? This, in fact, is the real ignorance. Besides, ours is not a qigong practice, but the Buddha Fa cultivation practice. Isn't any pressure a test to see whether your faith in the Buddha Fa is fundamentally strong? If you still are not fundamentally resolute in the Fa, everything else is out of question.

Li Hongzhi
December 21, 1995

The Buddha Fa's Terminology

Some practitioners once were lay Buddhists and have a very deep impression from the terms in Buddhist scriptures. When they find that I use words identical to those in Buddhism, they consider them to have the same meanings as those in Buddhism. In fact, they do not denote exactly the same meanings. Some terms in the Buddhism of the Han region are Chinese vocabulary, and they are not exclusively terms from Buddhism.

The key point is that these practitioners still cannot relinquish the things in Buddhism since they do not realize that their impressions from Buddhism still affect their minds, nor do they have a sufficient understanding of practicing no second cultivation school. Actually, isn't the superficial similarity one perceives causing interference? If you misinterpreted my words, wouldn't you be practicing cultivation in Buddhism?

Li Hongzhi
December 21, 1995

Pacifying the External by Cultivating the Internal

If man does not value virtue, the world will be in great chaos and out of control; everyone will become enemies of one another and live without happiness. Living without happiness, they will not fear death. Lao Zi said, "If the populace fears no death, what good would it do to threaten them with death?" This is a great, imminent danger. A peaceful world is what people hope for. If at this point an excessive number of laws and decrees are created to secure stability, the result will only turn out to be the opposite. To eliminate this concern, cultivating virtue around the world is the fundamental remedy. If officials are unselfish, the state will not be corrupt. If the population values self-cultivation and the nurturing of virtues, and if both administrators and civilians exercise self-restraint in their minds, the whole nation will be stable and supported by the people. Being solid and stable, the nation will automatically intimidate foreign enemies and peace will thus reign under heaven. This is the work of a sage.

Li Hongzhi
January 5, 1996

Further Elimination of Attachments

My disciples! Master is very worried, but this cannot help! Why can't you give up an everyday person's mindset? Why are you so reluctant to take a step forward? Our practitioners, including our staff, are jealous of each other even in their work for Dafa. Can you become a Buddha like this? I want to have a loose administration simply because you cannot give up things of everyday people and will thus feel uneasy in your work. Dafa belongs to the entire universe, and not to any one, insignificant individual. Whoever does the work is spreading Dafa. It is not important whether it should be done by you or by others. Are you going to bring to a paradise this attachment that you cannot give up, and contend with Buddhas? Nobody should treat Dafa as his or her own exclusive thing. Give up your

31

attachment of feeling injustice in your heart! When in your mind you cannot get over something, isn't it caused by your attachment? Our practitioners should not think that they are above that attachment! I hope that everyone will examine himself or herself, because you are all cultivators, with the exception of me, Li Hongzhi. Everyone should think about it: Why do I teach such a great Fa in the time of Last Havoc? If I disclose the truth, I will be teaching an evil practice since there will definitely be those who learn the Fa because of this. That is studying the Fa with pursuits. When saving people, the only way for them to get rid of their attachments is by having the right intention. It is known to all that one will not succeed in one's cultivation without giving up attachments. Why do you dare not abandon more and go one step further? In fact, there must be an unspeakable reason for my teaching this Dafa. Once the truth is revealed, it will be too late to regret. I have seen the attachments in some of you, but I cannot tell you directly. If I did, you would keep Master's words in mind and become attached to them for the rest of your life. I do not wish to ruin even one of my disciples. Saving people is indeed very difficult, and their enlightening is even more difficult. More importantly, everyone should carefully examine himself or herself in this light. You all know that Dafa is good, so why can't you give up your attachments?

Li Hongzhi
January 6, 1996

Verification

The Buddha Fa can save mankind, but it is not for the salvation of human beings that the Buddha Fa came into existence. The Buddha Fa can unravel the mysteries of the universe, life, and science. It enables mankind to resume the correct path in science, but it is not for the guidance of mankind's science that the Buddha Fa has been brought forth.

The Buddha Fa is the nature of the universe. It is the factor that created the origin of matter, and it is the reason for the genesis of the universe.

In the future there will then be many experts and scholars whose wisdom will be broadened through the Buddha Fa. They will become the new mankind's pioneers in different fields of learning. Yet it is not for you to become a pioneer that the Buddha Fa has given you wisdom. You have attained it because you are a cultivator. That is, you are first a cultivator and then an expert. Then, as a cultivator, you should make use of all feasible conditions to spread Dafa and verify that Dafa is correct and a genuine science, rather than preaching or idealism—this is every cultivator's obligation. Without this enormous Buddha Fa there would be nothing, including everything in the universe, from the most macroscopic to the most microscopic, as well as all of human society's knowledge.

Li Hongzhi
January 8, 1996

A Cultivator is Naturally Part of It

For a cultivator, all the frustrations he comes across among everyday people are trials, and all the compliments he receives are tests.

Li Hongzhi
January 14, 1996

What is Forbearance (Ren)?

Forbearance is the key to improving one's xinxing. To endure with anger, grievance, or tears is the forbearance of an everyday person who is attached to his concerns.

To endure completely without anger or grievance is a cultivator's forbearance.

Li Hongzhi
January 21, 1996

What is Mi Xin?[2]

Chinese people today really turn pale merely at the mentioning of the two characters "mi xin," because many people call everything that they do not believe "mi xin." In fact, these two characters, mi xin, were coated with an ultra "leftist" garb during the "Great Cultural Revolution," and they were used at that time as the most damaging term against the national culture. Being the most horrifying label, it has become the most irresponsible pet phrase of those simple-minded and stubborn people. Even those self-proclaimed, so-called "materialists" label everything beyond their knowledge or beyond the understanding of science as "mi xin." If things were to have been understood according to that theory, mankind would not have made any advancements; neither would science have developed further, because all of science's new progressions and

---

[2] mi xin (mee sheen)—"superstition," or "blind faith."

discoveries have been beyond the understanding of its predecessors. Then aren't these people themselves practicing idealism? Once human beings believe in something, isn't that, itself infatuation? Isn't it true that some people's trust in modern science or modern medicine is also mi xin? Isn't it true that people's revering their idols is mi xin as well? Actually, the two characters, mi xin, form a very common term. Once people zealously believe in something—including the truth—it becomes mi xin; it does not denote any derogatory meaning. It is only that when those with ulterior motives launch their attacks on others that they coat "mi xin" with the connotation of feudalism,[3] and thus it has become a very misleading and combatative term that can further incite simple-minded people to echo it.

As a matter of fact, the two characters, mi xin, themselves should not be used this way, neither should the imposed connotation exist. What the two characters, mi xin, imply is not anything negative. Without mi xin in discipline, soldiers would not have combatative capabilities; without mi xin in their schools and teachers, students would not acquire knowledge; without mi xin in their parents, children would not be brought up well-

---

[3] "feudalism"—in contemporary Mainland China, this is a very negative term that connotes backwardness and superstition.

mannered; without mi xin in their careers, people would not do a good job in their work; without beliefs, human beings would have no moral standards, the human mind would not have good thoughts, and it would be overcome by evil thoughts. At such a time, human moral values would decline rapidly. Possessed by evil thoughts, everyone would become enemies of one another and would stop at nothing to satisfy their selfish desires. Although those bad people who have imposed negative connotations on the two characters of "mi xin" have achieved their objectives, they have very likely ruined mankind in terms of its original nature.

Li Hongzhi
January 22, 1996
Revised on August 29, 1996

Sickness Karma

Why would a new practitioner who has just begun studying the practice, or a veteran practitioner whose body has been adjusted, experience physical discomfort in his cultivation practice as though he were seriously ill? Also, why does this happen once in a while? In teaching the Fa, I told you that this is to eliminate your karma and to improve your enlightenment quality while eliminating the karma from your different previous lives. Besides, this is also to test whether you are determined in following Dafa; this will continue until your cultivation reaches beyond Shi-Jian-Fa. This is putting it in general terms.

As a matter of fact, a person does not know how many lifetimes—in each of which he has accrued a great deal of karma—he has gone through. When a person is reincarnated after death, some of his sickness-karma is pressed into his body at the microscopic level. When he is reincarnated, the new physical body's matter has no sickness-karma on the surface (but there are exceptions for those with too much karma). What was pressed into the body in the previous life then comes out, and when it returns to the surface of this physical body, the person will become ill. Yet the sickness will usually appear to be triggered by an external condition in the physical world. This way it will conform on the surface to the objective laws of our physical world. That is, it will comply with this human world's principles. As a result, everyday people have no way of knowing the actual truth about the cause of the sickness, and they are thus lost in delusion without being enlightened. Upon becoming ill, the person will take medicine or seek various kinds of treatments that in effect press the sickness back into the body again. Consequently, instead of paying for the sickness-karma from his wrongdoing in the previous life, he will do some additional bad things in this life to hurt others; this will bring about new sickness-karma and lead to different kinds of sicknesses. Nevertheless, one will again take medicine or use various treatments to press the sickness back into the body. Surgery can only remove flesh in the superficial physical dimension, while the sickness-karma in another dimension has not been touched at all—it is simply beyond the reach of modern medical technology. When the sickness recurs, the person will again seek treatment. When a person is reincarnated after death, any sickness-karma that has accrued will again be pressed back into his body. This cycle goes on one lifetime after another; it is unknown how much sickness-karma accumulates in a person's body. This is why I said that all of today's mankind has come to this point with karma built upon karma; besides sickness-karma, a person has other kinds of karma as well. Therefore, people have hardships, tribulations, and conflicts in their lives. How can they only pursue happiness without paying for karma? People nowadays have so much karma that they are soaked in it, and they will encounter unpleasant things at any time and in any situation. Whenever a person leaves his home, there will be something bad awaiting him. When there are conflicts, however, people do not endure them and do not realize that they are paying off their karma from the past. If a person is not treated well by others, he will treat others even worse, thereby producing new karma before paying for the old. This makes society's moral values decline daily, and everyone becomes enemies among one another. Many people cannot think through this: What's happened to people today? What's going on with today's society? If mankind continues like this, it will be extremely dangerous!

As a cultivator, in addition to the karma eliminated by Master, you have to pay for a portion yourself. You will thus feel physically uncomfortable, as though you were suffering from a sickness. Cultivation practice is to clean you up from the origin of your life. The human body is like the annual rings of a tree, whereby each ring contains sickness-karma. So your body must be cleaned up from the very center. Were karma to be pushed out all at once, however, you would not be able to take it, for it would endanger your life. Only a piece or two can be pushed out every once in a while, allowing you to overcome it, and through the suffering pay off your karma. But this is only that little bit left for you, yourself to endure after I have eliminated karma for you. This will continue until your cultivation reaches the highest form of Shi-Jian-Fa (i.e., the pure-white body), when all of your karma will have been pushed out. Yet there are also some people with very little sickness-karma, and there are other special cases. Cultivation practice in Beyond Shi-Jian-Fa is that of the purest Arhat body—a body that does not have any sickness-karma. But as for a person that has not yet achieved completion of cultivation and who is still practicing cultivation towards higher levels beyond Shi-Jian-Fa, he will still suffer and have tribulations and trials to advance his level. These will only involve interpersonal conflicts or those involving other things in the area of xinxing and the further abandonment of his attachments; he will no longer have physical sickness-karma.

Eliminating sickness-karma is a matter that cannot be casually done for an everyday person, and this is absolutely impossible for a non-practitioner that must only rely on medical treatment. Doing this at will for an everyday person is actually undermining the principles of heaven, for it means that a person can do bad things without having to pay for the karma. It absolutely will not do if a person does not repay his debts—the principles of heaven won't permit it! Even the treatments of ordinary qigong also are to push the karma inside a person's body. When a person has too much karma and is still doing bad things, he will face destruction—the complete destruction of both body and soul—at his death, which is total extinction. When treating a sickness for a human being, a great enlightened being can completely eliminate the karmic cause of that sickness, but this is done mainly with the purpose of saving people.

Li Hongzhi
March 10, 1996

Cultivators' Avoidances

Full of intention, those who are attached to fame practice an evil way. Once fame in this world is achieved, they are bound to say good but mean evil, thereby misleading the public and undermining the Fa.

Those who are attached to money seek wealth and fake their cultivation. Undermining the practice and the Fa, they waste their lifetimes instead of cultivating Buddhahood.

Those who are attached to lust are no different from wicked people. While reciting the scriptures, they even cast furtive glances; they are quite far from the Tao and are wicked, everyday people.

Those who are attached to affection for family will definitely be burned, entangled, and tormented by it.

Grabbed by the threads of affection and plagued by them throughout their lives, they will find it too late to regret at the end of their lives.

Li Hongzhi
April 15, 1996

Perfect Harmony

(I.)

In different workplace environments, people are involved in different aspects of killing. The balance of lives manifests in different forms. As a cultivator, you should first of all give up all attachments and conform to the state of human society, as this is maintaining the Fa's manifestation at a certain level. If no one performs the human jobs, the Fa at this level will cease to exist.

(II.)

Lives exist or die naturally within the Fa. The universe goes through formation, settlement, and degeneration, and human beings undergo birth, old age, illness, and death. There also exist unnatural births or deaths in the balance of lives. There is sacrifice in forbearance, and a complete sacrifice is a higher principle of non-omission.

Li Hongzhi
April 19, 1996

Non-Omission

There is sacrifice in forbearance. Being able to make sacrifices is an upgrade in one's cultivation practice. The Fa has different levels. A cultivator's understanding of the Fa is his understanding of the Fa at his cultivation level. Different cultivators understand the Fa differently because they are at different levels.

For cultivators at different levels, the Fa has different requirements. Sacrifice is evidenced by one's being detached from an everyday person's attachment. If a person can indeed calmly abandon everything with his heart being unmoved, he is actually at that level already. Yet cultivation practice is to upgrade yourself: You are already able to give up the attachment, so why not give up the fear of attachment, itself as well? Isn't abandonment without omission a higher sacrifice? Yet if a cultivator or an everyday person who cannot even make fundamental sacrifices also discusses this principle, he is actually undermining the Fa by making an excuse for the attachment he cannot give up.

Li Hongzhi
April 26, 1996

Cultivation and Work

With the exception of professional cultivators in temples, the vast majority of our Falun Dafa practitioners are practicing cultivation in ordinary human society. Through studying and practicing Dafa, all of you can take fame and self-interest lightly. Yet, a lack of in-depth understanding of the Fa has given rise to a problem: A small number of disciples have given up their jobs among everyday people or refuse to be promoted to leadership positions. This has incurred much unnecessary interference in their work and lives, directly affecting their cultivation practice. Some decent business people think that they have taken money lightly and, at the same time, that doing business may harm others and affect their own cultivation practice. They have also given up their business.

In fact, Dafa's content is very profound. Abandoning an everyday person's mindset does not mean giving up an everyday person's job. Giving up fame and self-interest is not to distance yourself from ordinary human society. I have repeatedly pointed it out that those who practice cultivation in ordinary human society must conform to the state of ordinary human society.

Viewed from another perspective, if all leadership positions in ordinary human society were taken by people like us who can let go of their personal fame and self-interest, what great benefits would it bring to people? And what would be brought to society if a very greedy person were to come into power? If all business people were cultivators of Dafa, what would society's morality be like?

The Dafa of the universe (the Buddha Fa) is coherent and complete from the highest level to the lowest level. You should know that ordinary human society is also composed of a level of the Fa. If everyone were to study Dafa and give up their jobs in society, ordinary human society would cease to exist and so would this level of the Fa. Ordinary human society is the manifestation of the Fa at the lowest level, and it is also the form of existence of life and matter for the Buddha Fa at this level.

Li Hongzhi
April 26, 1996

Correction

At present, practitioners in different regions take the following, put forward by the Research Society, as the Fa or my words to spread and study:

> Read Dafa selectively,
> Cultivate your xinxing sincerely,
> Practice the exercises arduously… etc.

Actually, they are not my words, nor do they have a deeper meaning—they are certainly not the Fa. What is meant by "selective reading" differs greatly from my requirement in studying the Fa. As a matter of fact, I was very explicit about reading the books in the article, "Studying the Fa," that I wrote on September 9, 1995. Besides, what is meant by "intensive reading" has caused serious interference with "Studying the Fa." From now on you must pay attention to the seriousness of this problem. I have talked about the reason why Buddhism disappeared in India and its lesson. If no caution is taken in the future, it will be the beginning of the disruption of the Fa. Attention: When a problem arises, do not try to find out who should take responsibility. One should, instead, examine one's own conduct. Do not try to look into who wrote them. Take a lesson from it and be careful in the future.

Li Hongzhi
April 28, 1996

Durability

To keep Dafa unchanged forever, it seems that there still exists a problem: That is, there are always practitioners who—driven by their mentality of showing off and the intention of being different—will do things that interfere with Dafa once an opportunity arises. This can be very serious sometimes. For example, recently someone has been saying that I have individually taught a practitioner the essentials of the exercises (the fact is that I only corrected a practitioner's movements when he asked me). That has thus invalidated the exercise movements I have been teaching in different regions for the past few years. While I am still around and under the circumstance that the instructional videotape is still available, this person even publicly altered Dafa's exercise movements. He told the practitioners not to practice according to the videotape but to follow him, claiming that Teacher has high-level gong, is different from his students, and so on. He also told the practitioners to practice according to their own conditions first, to gradually make the changes in the future, and the like.

From the very beginning I have taught the exercises in their entirety, because I was concerned that some practitioners might make arbitrary changes. Once the energy mechanism forms, it can never be changed. The matter may seem insignificant, but it is actually the beginning of a serious disruption of the Fa. Some people take the transitional movements as individual ones and tell practitioners to do them in a standardized way. Doing such is trying to be different. This has brought about very serious effects in different regions at the present time. My disciples! My instructional videotapes are still available—why would you follow these people so readily?! Dafa is the solemn, great Fa of the universe. Even if you disrupt just a bit of it, what a mammoth sin it is! As a cultivator, you should practice cultivation in an open and dignified manner and look at the larger picture. How can it be possible that everyone's movements are exactly the same, without any slight differences? Don't focus your mind on such trivialities. The exercise movements are a way to help complete one's cultivation—and they are certainly important, but instead of digging into a bullhorn's tip, you should devote more effort to improving your xinxing. In fact, most interference for Dafa comes internally, from practitioners themselves. External factors can only affect a few individuals and cannot alter the Fa. Whether at present or in the future, those who can undermine our Fa will be no one but practitioners themselves. Do be careful! Our Fa is unchangeable and eternal. No one can use any excuses for any reason or under any circumstance to alter even a bit of the movements with which we are to complete cultivation. Otherwise, this person is undermining the Fa, regardless of whether his motives are good or not.

Li Hongzhi
May 11, 1996

Do Not Make Wild Statements

Recently an expression has been circulating. That is, when practitioners spread Dafa, thereby helping some people with predestined relationships to obtain the Fa and begin their cultivation practice, these practitioners claim that they have saved people. They say, "Today I saved a few people, and you saved several people," and so on. Actually, it is the Fa that saves people, and only Master can do such a thing. You have only helped people with predestined relationships obtain the Fa. Whether they can truly be saved still depends on whether they can complete their cultivation. Do be careful: Once such wild statements are made—intentionally or not—even a Buddha will be shocked. Don't create obstacles for your own cultivation practice. You must also cultivate your speech in this respect. I hope you can understand.

Li Hongzhi
May 21, 1996

Awakening

The time for genuine Dafa cultivation is limited. Many practitioners have realized that they must hurry up and diligently make continual progress. Yet some practitioners do not treasure their time, and focus their minds on tangential issues. Since this book of Dafa, <u>Zhuan Falun</u>, was published, many people have compared the recordings of my lectures with the book, claiming that the Research Society changed Teacher's words. Some others said that the book was written with the help of so-and-so, thereby undermining Dafa. I am telling you now that Dafa belongs to me, Li Hongzhi. It is taught to save you and spoken from my mouth. Additionally, when I taught the Fa, I did not use any scripts or other materials, but only a piece of paper

51

concerning what I would teach to my students; it contained something very simple with only a few points that no one else could understand. Every time I taught the Fa I presented it from a different angle and delivered my speech according to the students' ability to comprehend. Therefore, every time I taught the Fa I would address the same issue from different angles. Furthermore, this book of the Fa represents the characteristic of the universe and is the true manifestation of the mighty Buddha Fa. It is what I originally had, that which I recalled after attaining enlightenment through cultivation practice. I then made it public in everyday people's language, and I taught it to you as well as to those in heavens, thereby rectifying the universe with the Fa. For the convenience of learners' cultivation practice, I assigned some students to transcribe the contents of my lectures from the tape recordings without any changes to my original words; they then gave it to me for revision. The students merely copied my revisions or typed it on a computer so that I could make further revisions. As far as <u>Zhuan Falun</u> is concerned, it was finalized and published after I personally revised it three times.

No one has ever made even a slight change regarding the content of this book of Dafa. Furthermore, who could possibly do that? There are three reasons for its differences from the tape recordings. First, for the convenience of cultivation practice, in the revision I have incorporated many of my lectures on the Fa. Secondly, while giving the lectures on the Fa, I taught it according to students' different abilities to comprehend and on the situations and circumstances at that time; therefore, I had to modify the structure of the language when editing it into a book. Thirdly, when cultivators study it, misunderstandings can occur due to the differences between the speech and the written language, so modification was needed. Nonetheless, the form and colloquial style of my lectures on the Fa were still preserved. <u>Zhuan Falun (Volume Two)</u>, and <u>Falun Dafa Explication</u>, were also personally revised by me before they were published. I incorporated thinking at different levels in writing <u>Zhuan Falun (Volume Two)</u>, so some people find the writing style different and are puzzled by it. These are not things of everyday people to begin with! In fact, <u>Volume Two</u> is reserved for future generations to learn the extent of mankind's degeneration today, thereby leaving people a profound historical lesson. <u>China Falun Gong,</u> including its revised version, is only a transitional material in the form of qigong for people to understand at the beginning.

The disruption of the Fa takes many forms, of which

the unintentional disruption by disciples themselves is the most difficult to detect. Sakyamuni's Buddhism began its deterioration in just this way and the lesson is profound.

Disciples must remember: All Falun Dafa texts are the Fa that I have taught, and they are revised and edited personally by me. From now on, no one may take excerpts from the tape recordings of my lectures on the Fa, or compile them into written materials. Regardless of any excuses you may have, it is undermining the Fa; this includes the so-called "contrasting the differences between the speech and its written form," and so on.

Nothing in the evolution of cosmic bodies or mankind's development is accidental. Human society's development is directed by history and is driven by the cosmic climate. In the future, there will be more people around the world learning Dafa. This is not something that can be done by a hot-headed person simply because he wants to. For such a major event, how can there not be various arrangements in history? Actually, everything that I have done was arranged innumerous years ago, and this includes those who have obtained the Fa— nothing is accidental; but these things manifest in the same forms as those of everyday people. As a matter of fact, the things imparted to me by my several masters in this life are also what I intentionally arranged a few lifetimes ago for them to obtain. When the predestined occasion arrived, they were arranged to impart those things back to me so as to enable me to recall my Fa in its entirety. So let me tell you that this book of the Fa is not only studied by the level of human beings, but also by the beings at higher levels. It is because a very large scope of the cosmic body has deviated from the fundamental nature of the universe that it has to be rectified by the Fa. Mankind is rather insignificant in the vast universe. Earth is nothing in the cosmos but a speck of dust. If human beings want to be valued by higher beings, they must practice cultivation and become higher beings as well!

Li Hongzhi
May 27, 1996

Stability of the Fa

In the past two years, some problems have occurred in practitioners' cultivation practice. I have been observing the situation of practitioners' cultivation practice. To correct the rising problems promptly, I often intentionally write some short articles (called "scriptures" by practitioners) to guide practitioners in their cultivation practice. The purpose is to leave a stable, healthy, and correct way for Dafa cultivation practice. The future generations for thousands of years to come must follow in their cultivation the way I have personally left if they are to complete their cultivation.

Recently, however, I saw a collection of materials at a practice site in Hong Kong that were passed there from another region; two of the materials were short articles not intended for publication. This was a serious and intentional act of undermining Dafa! Even transcribing them from tape recordings without permission still isn't right! I have made it clear in the article "Awakening" that there is no excuse for anybody's transcribing my words into written materials from the tape recordings—doing this is undermining the Fa. Meanwhile, I have repeatedly emphasized that you cannot circulate the private notes that you took during my lectures. Why do you still do that? What mentality drove you to write them? Let me tell you that except the several officially published books of mine and the dated short articles with my signature that are distributed to different regions by the Research Society, everything transcribed without permission is undermining the Fa. Cultivation is your own matter, and it is your own decision as to what you pursue. All everyday people have both demon-nature and Buddha-nature. Once one's mind is not right, demon-nature will come into play. Let me tell you once again that an outsider can never undermine the Fa. Only practitioners can undermine the Fa—remember this!

Every step I, Li Hongzhi, take is to establish an unchangeable and unalterable way for the dissemination of Dafa in future generations. Such an enormous Fa will not be over after momentary popularity. There cannot be any slight deviation in the countless years to come. Protecting Dafa with your own conduct is forever the responsibility of Dafa disciples, because Dafa belongs to all sentient beings of the universe, and this includes you.

Li Hongzhi
June 11, 1996

Cultivation Practice and Taking Responsibility

Being diligent in genuine cultivation is to complete cultivation within the shortest time possible. A practitioner is simply one who eliminates the attachments of an everyday person. Disciples, you must be clear about what you're doing!

To be responsible to Dafa, the assistance centers, general

assistance centers in different regions, and the Research Society have the right to replace any assistant or person in charge of a branch. Therefore, at times, a person in a position of responsibility may be replaced based on varying situations. Because a person in charge is, first of all, a practitioner who has come here for cultivation practice rather than for being in charge, he should be able to move up and down in his position. Being assigned a position with responsibility is for cultivation practice, yet one can practice cultivation all the same without being in a responsible position. If the person being replaced cannot get over it in his heart, isn't that caused by his attachment? Isn't it a good opportunity for him to get rid of that attachment? Given this, if he still cannot give up this attachment, this clearly indicates that it is correct to make the replacement. An attachment to being in a position of responsibility is in itself an unjustified motive for cultivation practice. So let me remind disciples: you will not be able to complete cultivation without giving up this attachment.

Li Hongzhi
June 12, 1996

Disposal of Handwritten Copies of Scriptures

At present, more and more people are learning Dafa, and the number is doubling on a weekly basis. Because the publishers' book supply are inadequate, they cannot meet the demand. The books are thus unavailable in some regions or in the countryside. Some practitioners have asked me what to do with their handwritten copies of Dafa. Let me tell you that for the time being you can give the copies of <u>Zhuan Falun</u> or other scriptures you have handwritten during your study of Dafa to those who will go to the rural areas to spread the practice and the Fa; bringing them to farmers can, at the same time, lessen their economic burdens. Therefore, this requires that practitioners' handwritten copies be legible so that farmers with limited education can understand them. Handwritten copies have the same power of the Fa as the printed books.

Li Hongzhi
June 26, 1996

The Fa Conference

It is very necessary for the disciples to share with one another what they have experienced and learned in their cultivation practice. There is no problem with them helping one another make progress together, so long as they have no intention of showing themselves off. To facilitate the dissemination of Dafa, some conferences for sharing cultivation experiences have been held in different regions. All of these conferences are very good and healthy—both in format and content. But the practitioners' speeches must be approved by the assistance centers to avoid political issues, which have nothing to do with cultivation practice, or issues that set incorrect trends in cultivation practice and in society. Meanwhile, we should avoid practicing superficial boasting—something which derives from everyday people's theoretical studies.[4] Compiling articles like submitted documents to be read with the intention of showing oneself off is not permitted.

Big conferences for sharing cultivation experiences that are organized by the general assistance centers at the provincial or city level should not be held on a national scale. A national or an international one should be organized by the Research Society, and they should not be held too frequently. Once a year should be good (except for special cases). Do not turn them into a formality or competition; instead, make it a solemn Fa conference that can truly advance one's cultivation

[4] See note no. 1

practice.

Li Hongzhi
June 26, 1996

A Letter to Shijiazhuang Dafa General Assistance Center

Shijiazhuang Dafa General Assistance Center:

I have learned that your conference for sharing cultivation experiences met with obstacles. There were three reasons for that, and you will certainly learn a lesson from it. In fact, this incident has directly affected the Dafa activities in Beijing and the entire country, and it will have a certain negative impact on normal Dafa activities later on. I think that you will definitely realize this and do better in the future.

Additionally, let me say a few more words about Jing Zhanyi's speeches at the seminar conference. Jing Zhanyi's situation is for the validation of Dafa's scientific nature from science's perspective, thereby letting the scientific and technological community or the academic world come to understand Dafa. He was not supposed to give speeches to practitioners, as doing so would not do any good at all and would only cause new practitioners or disciples without a solid understanding of the Fa to develop attachments. But without needing to listen to such speeches, those disciples who study the Fa well will continue their determined cultivation in Dafa all the same.

More importantly, I have taught the Fa for two years, and I have given disciples two years to genuinely practice cultivation. Over disciples' two years of genuine cultivation, I have not allowed any activities that have nothing to do with genuine cultivation to interfere with the orderly and step-by-step processes of improvement arranged for practitioners. If the speeches are not given to the scientific and academic communities to validate the scientific nature of Dafa, but rather to the cultivating disciples who have limited time, think about it: could there be a greater interference with practitioners than that? In order not to disturb practitioners, I do not even see them. If practitioners see me, they cannot calm down for at least a few days, and this disrupts the arrangements I had my fashen make for them. I have told the Research Society about this issue, but perhaps it was not made clear to Jing Zhanyi. Now that the matter is over, none of you should try to determine who should be held accountable. I think that the main reason [for this] is that you did not realize it. But you must pay attention from now on. Everything we do today is to lay a foundation for future dissemination of Dafa over countless years to come, and to leave a perfect, correct, and error-free form of cultivation practice. Today I point this out not to criticize anyone, but to correct the form of cultivation practice—[a form which is] to be left for future generations.

This letter is to be distributed to the assistance centers in different regions.

Li Hongzhi
June 26, 1996

Rectification of One's Character

With progress in genuine cultivation in Dafa, many disciples have successively attained enlightenment or achieved gradual enlightenment. They can see the actual, splendid, and magnificent scenes in other dimensions. The disciples experiencing the process of enlightenment are so excited that they call my fashen the "second master," or take my fashen as a true and independent master—this is a misunderstanding. Fashen is the manifest image of my omnipresent wisdom, but not an independent living being. Some other disciples call Falun "Master Falun." This is absolutely, grossly wrong. Falun is another manifest form of my Fa power's nature and Dafa's wisdom—things too wonderful to be described with words. Falun is the manifestation of the nature of the Fa of all matter in the universe, from the macroscopic level to the microscopic level, and it is not an independent living being.

When you see my fashen and Falun doing those great, miraculous, and magnificent things for you, you disciples must remember not to view or compliment my fashen or Falun with the mind of an everyday person. Such a mindset is a mixed expression of very poor enlightenment quality and very poor xinxing. As a matter of fact, all manifesting forms are the concrete manifestations of my using the enormous power of the Fa to rectify the Fa and save people.

Li Hongzhi
July 2, 1996

A Brief Explanation of Compassion *(Shan)*

Shan is the manifestation of the cosmos' quality at different levels and in different dimensions. It is also the fundamental nature of the great enlightened beings.

Therefore, a cultivator must cultivate Shan and become assimilated to the cosmos' quality, Zhen-Shan-Ren. The vast cosmic body was born of the cosmos' quality, Zhen-Shan-Ren. Dafa's public teaching has re-demonstrated the past, primordial nature of the living beings of the universe. Dafa is in perfect harmony. Taking the three characters of "Zhen-Shan-Ren" apart, each still fully contains Zhen-Shan-Ren. This is because matter is composed of microscopic matter, which, in turn, is made up of even more microscopic matter—this goes on and on until the end. Therefore, Zhen consists of Zhen-Shan-Ren, Shan consists of Zhen-Shan-Ren, and Ren also consists of Zhen-Shan-Ren. Isn't the cultivation of Zhen by the Tao School the cultivation of Zhen-Shan-Ren? Isn't the cultivation of Shan by the Buddha School also the cultivation of Zhen-Shan-Ren? In actuality, they only differ in their superficial forms.

In terms of Shan alone, when it manifests in human society, some everyday people who are attached to ordinary human society may raise a social question of everyday people, saying, "If everyone learns Dafa and practices Shan, what if foreign invasions against us or wars take place?" In fact, I have already said in <u>Zhuan Falun</u> that the development of human society is driven by the evolution of the cosmic climate. Are the wars of mankind accidental, then? A region with a lot of karma

65

or a region where human hearts have become corrupt is bound to be unstable. If one nationality is truly virtuous, it must have little karma; there absolutely will be no wars occurring against it. This is because this is prohibited by the principle of Dafa, as the quality of the universe governs everything. One needs not worry that a virtuous nation will be invaded. The characteristic of the universe—Dafa—is present everywhere, encompassing the entire cosmic body, from the macroscopic level to the microscopic level. As to the Dafa that I am teaching today, it is taught not only to Eastern people, but also at the same time to Western people. Their good-natured people should also be saved. All nationalities that should enter the next, new historical era will obtain the Fa and improve as a whole. It is not just a matter of one nationality. Mankind's moral standard will also return to that of original human nature.

Li Hongzhi
July 20, 1996

Annotation on "Rectification of One's Character"

After I said that "fashen and Falun are not independent living beings," some practitioners asked whether this is contradictory to what is stated in <u>Zhuan Falun</u>: "Fashen's

66

consciousness and thoughts are controlled by the person. Yet fashen itself is also a complete, independent, and actual individual being." I think that this is due to a lack of good understanding of the Fa. Fashen cannot be understood as the same concept of those completely independent lives, because fashen are the willed manifestations of the power and wisdom of the master person's image and thoughts; they are capable of accomplishing anything independently, according to the will of the master person. So the practitioners only noticed the second sentence while overlooking the first one: "Fashen's consciousness and thoughts are controlled by the master person." Fashen thus does not only have the independent and complete image of the master person, but also the character and characteristics of the master person; it can also independently accomplish everything the master person would want to, whereas an ordinary life is controlled by no one. When people look at fashen, they will find it a complete, independent, and realistic individual life. In fact, to put it plainly, my fashen is just myself.

Li Hongzhi
July 21, 1996

Buddha-Nature and Demon-Nature

In a very high and very microscopic dimension of the universe, there exist two different kinds of substances. They are two forms of material existence manifest by the supreme characteristic of the universe—Zhen-Shan-Ren, at certain levels of dimensions in the universe. They pervade certain dimensions from the top to the bottom or from the microscopic level to the macroscopic level. With regard to the Fa's manifestations at different levels, the lower the level, the greater the difference in the manifestations and variations of these two different kinds of substances. As a result, it brings forth what the Tao School calls the principles of Yin-Yang and Taiji. Descending further to lower levels, these two kinds of matter, with different properties, become increasingly opposed to each other, and this then gives rise to the principle of inter-generation and inter-inhibition.

Through inter-generation and inter-inhibition there appear kindness and malevolence, right and wrong, and good and evil. Then, as to living beings, if there are Buddhas, there are demons; if there are humans, there are ghosts—this is more obvious and complicated in ordinary human society. Where there are good people, there are bad ones; where there are selfless people, there are selfish ones; where there are open-minded people, there are narrow-minded ones. In terms of cultivation practice, where there are people who believe in it, there are people who do not; where there are people who can be enlightened, there are people who cannot; where there are people for it, there are people against it—this is human society. If everyone could practice cultivation, be enlightened to it, and believe in it, human society would turn into a society of gods. Human society is simply a society of human beings, and it is not allowed to cease to exist. Human society will continue to exist forever. Therefore, it is normal that there are people who oppose it; if, instead, no one objected, it would be abnormal. Without ghosts, how could humans be incarnated into humans? Without the existence of demons, one would be unable to cultivate Buddhahood. Without bitterness, there could not be sweetness.

Precisely because of the existing principle of inter-generation and inter-inhibition, people will come across difficulty when trying to accomplish something. Only when you succeed in accomplishing what you want by making bitter efforts and overcoming difficulties will you find it not easily won, cherish what you have achieved, and feel happy. Otherwise, if there were no principle of inter-generation and inter-inhibition and you could effortlessly accomplish anything, you would feel bored with life, without a sense of happiness or the joy of success.

Any kind of matter or life in the universe is composed of microscopic particles that make up larger particles, and these then form surface matter. Within the scope covered by these two kinds of matter of differing properties, all matter and lives possess dual nature just the same. For instance, iron and steel are very hard, but they will become oxidized and rusty when buried in the earth. Pottery and porcelain, on the other hand, will not become oxidized when buried in the earth, but they are very fragile and can be easily broken. The same applies to human beings, who possess Buddha-nature and demon-nature at the same time. What one does without moral obligations and constraints is of the demon-nature. Cultivating Buddhahood is to eliminate your demon-nature and solidify your Buddha-nature.

One's Buddha-nature is Shan, and it manifests itself as compassion, thinking of others before doing anything, and the ability to endure sufferings. One's demon-nature is viciousness, and it manifests itself as killing, stealing and robbing, selfishness, evil thoughts, sowing discord, stirring up troubles by spreading rumors, jealousy, wickedness, anger, laziness, incest and so on.

Being the characteristic of the cosmos, Zhen-Shan-Ren

manifests differently at different levels. The two different kinds of substances within certain levels of the universe also have different manifesting forms at different levels. The lower the level, the more marked the inter-opposition, and thus the division between good and bad. The virtuous becomes more virtuous, while the evil becomes more evil. The dual nature in the same physical subject also becomes more complicated and changeable. This is exactly what Buddha stated: everything has Buddha-nature. As a matter of fact, everything has demon-nature as well.

Nevertheless, the universe is characterized by Zhen-Shan-Ren, and so is ordinary human society. The two kinds of substances I have mentioned are among numerous kinds of matter that exist from the top to the bottom, from the microscopic level to the macroscopic level, to until human society, and they are nothing but two kinds of dual nature producing substances that manifest in life and matter. But lives and matter from the top to the bottom until human society are composed of countless varieties of matter from the microscopic level to the macroscopic level.

If mankind does not observe human moral standards, society will be in uncontrollable chaos, with natural calamities and man-made disasters. If a cultivator does

71

not get rid of his demon-nature through cultivation, his gong will be messed up very badly and he will attain nothing or follow a demonic path.

Li Hongzhi
August 26, 1996

Big Exposure

At present, a large number of practitioners have achieved or are about to achieve the completion of cultivation. What a solemn event it is for a human being to complete cultivation! Nothing in this world could be more wonderful, glorious, or magnificent than this. That being the case, strict requirements must be imposed on every cultivator in the course of his cultivation practice. In addition, upgrading to each higher level should be based on the strict observance of the criteria. In terms of the overall situation, Dafa practitioners are up to standard, but there are also some people who are fumbling along with various attachments that they have not abandoned. Superficially, they, too, say that Dafa is good, but in reality they do not practice cultivation. Especially in the general climate where everyone says that Dafa is good, everyone, from the upper classes of society to the common people, speaks highly of it. Some governments also say good things that are echoed by the public. Who are the sincere ones, then? Who are merely echoing others' voices? Who sings its praises with their mouths while actually undermining it? We have changed the situation in human society and reversed the general climate: Let's see who still says that Dafa is good and who changes his mind. This way, hasn't everything suddenly become crystal clear?

From the incident with the *Guangming Daily* until now, every Dafa disciple has played a role: some are determined in their genuine cultivation; for the reputation of Dafa, some wrote without reservation to the authorities; some spoke out against the injustice done by the irresponsible report. But there were also some who, amidst the difficult situation, did not cultivate their inner selves, but engaged in divisive activities that further complicated the current situation. Some even stopped their cultivation, fearing that their personal reputations and interests would be harmed. Still others circulated rumors without any concern for the stability of Dafa, exacerbating factors that undermine the Fa. There were also a number of key contact persons in different regions who analyzed the situation of Dafa with the unhealthy habit of observing social trends that developed over years of political struggle. By relating isolated problems that arose in different regions, they concluded that some sorts of social trends were unfolding and they intentionally communicated this to practitioners. Despite there being various reasons for this, could there be a more serious disruption of the Fa than this? Even worse, some stirred up troubles by creating rumors with their demon-nature, as though the situation were not chaotic enough.

Dafa belongs to the universe and penetrates all the way down to human society. When such an enormous Fa is taught, how can there not be an arrangement made for everything? Isn't what has happened a test for Dafa disciples' xinxing? What is cultivation? When you say it is good, I say it is good, and everyone says it is good, how can one's heart be seen? Only at the critical moment can we see one's heart. Without giving up some of the attachments, one might even dare betray Buddha— could this be a minor problem? Some people were scared. But what were you afraid of? My disciples! Didn't you hear me mention that when a person succeeded in cultivating Arhatship, he stumbled because he developed fear in his heart? Every human attachment must be given up, no matter what it is. Some disciples said: "What's there to fear? My body will still be sitting there, even with my head off." In comparison, it only takes but one look to gauge one's cultivation. Of course, some key contact persons are concerned for the safety

74

of Dafa, and this is another story.

We just want to make those disciples who are not diligent in cultivation practice see their own shortcomings, make those who are stumbling along surface, expose those who undermine the Fa in disguised form, and let those genuine disciples reach completion.

Li Hongzhi
August 28, 1996

Cultivation Practice is Not Political

Some practitioners are discontented with society and politics; they have learned our Dafa with this strong attachment that they do not release. They even attempt to take advantage of our Dafa to get involved in politics—an act born of a filthy mentality, showing their irreverence toward Buddha and the Fa. Without giving up this mentality, they absolutely will not complete cultivation.

In my lectures I have repeatedly stressed that the form of human society—no matter what type of society or political situation—is predestined and determined by heaven. A cultivator does not need to mind the affairs of the human world, let alone get involved in political struggles. As to how society treats us, isn't it to test a cultivator's heart? We should not get involved in politics.

Such is our Dafa's form of cultivation practice. We will not rely on any political powers at home or abroad. Those people of influence are not cultivators, so they certainly cannot hold any positions with responsibilities in our Dafa—either in name or in actuality.

My disciples, you must remember that we are practicing genuine cultivation! We should let go of the fame, profits, and sentimentality of everyday people. Do the conditions of a social system have anything to do with your cultivation practice? Only after you have abandoned all of your attachments and none remain can you complete cultivation. Other than doing a good job with his work, a cultivator will not be interested in politics or any political power; otherwise, he is absolutely not my disciple.

We are able to have cultivators obtain the Fa and achieve the Righteous Fruit, just as we are able to teach people's hearts to be good in society—this is good for the stability of human society. Dafa is not, however, taught for the sake of human society, but for you to complete cultivation practice.

Li Hongzhi
September 3, 1996

A Person in Charge is Also a Cultivator

The persons in charge of our assistance centers in different regions are those who can all work hard for Dafa without complaint. Many of these persons, however, just cannot get along well with one another and consequently fail to cooperate in their work. This has greatly damaged Dafa's image in people's minds. Some have asked me whether this is because they are incapable of doing the work. I said that this is an everyday person's view. The crucial reason is that you, as directors and assistant directors of the centers, are cultivators who also have attachments that you cannot give up—you need an environment to get rid of them. But when a conflict arises among those in charge, you usually use the excuse "not cooperating in the work" or "working for Dafa" to push it aside, instead of taking advantage of this good opportunity to search within to improve yourself. As you did not give up your attachments or upgrade yourselves, the conflict will recur the next time. This will indeed interfere with the work for Dafa. Don't you know that the conflicts among those in charge are arranged by me for you to improve yourselves? Yet you use the work for Dafa to cover up your heart that you should have improved but did not. When the conflict becomes too serious to overcome, you grieve to me in your mind. Do you know how I feel about it at that time? It is not that simply because you are the director of a center and work for Dafa you can complete cultivation without having to improve your xinxing. Even a practitioner can realize that he is improving his xinxing within any conflict—why can't the director of a center? In order to enable your improvement, it will not do if your heart is not provoked when conflicts arise. Working for Dafa is also a good opportunity for you to improve your xinxing!

Why do I specifically write this article for you? This is because every act or every statement of yours will directly affect practitioners. If you are doing well in your cultivation, you will do well in spreading the Fa in your local area and practitioners will do better in their cultivation. Otherwise, you will cause damage to the Fa. As you are Dafa's elite at the level of everyday people, I cannot just let you work without completing cultivation.

Li Hongzhi

September 3, 1996

What is Cultivation Practice?

As to cultivation practice, many people believe that cultivation practice is only about doing some exercises, sitting in meditation, and learning some incantations that can then transform them into Gods or Buddhas or allow them to attain the Tao. In fact, this is not cultivation practice but merely practicing for worldly skills.

In religion, much attention has been directed at cultivation, and this is called conduct cultivation. Accordingly, it has gone to the other extreme. A monk or a nun tries very hard to chant the scriptures and regards one's depth in understanding of the scriptures as the means to completing cultivation. In fact, when Buddha Sakyamuni, Jesus, and Lao Zi were in this world, there were no scriptures at all—there was only genuine cultivation. What the venerable masters taught were statements made to guide cultivation practice. Recalling their words, later followers put them into books and called them scriptures. They gradually began to study Buddhist philosophy or the theories of Dharma. Unlike what happened during the days of the venerable masters—when people would genuinely practice cultivation and use their teachings as the guide for genuine cultivation, these people have instead taken the study of religious scriptures and scholarship as cultivation practice.

This is a lesson in history. The disciples who practice cultivation in Falun Dafa must remember that you absolutely should not take the Fa merely as the academic scholarship of everyday people or for monks to study rather than genuinely practicing cultivation. Why do I tell you to study, read, and memorize <u>Zhuan Falun</u>? It is to guide your cultivation practice! As to those who only do the exercises but do not study the Fa, they are not disciples of Dafa whatsoever. Only when you are studying the Fa and cultivating your heart in addition to the means of completing cultivation—the exercises, and truly changing yourself fundamentally while upgrading your xinxing and elevating your level—can it be called genuine cultivation practice.

Li Hongzhi
September 6, 1996

Dafa Will Forever be Pure Like Diamond

Religion cannot be mingled with politics; otherwise,

its leader will necessarily be preoccupied with worldly affairs. Paying lip service to teaching people's hearts to be good and leading people back to the pure land, his heart is bound to be evil and hypocritical; what he pursues will certainly be fame and self-interest. Power is what everyday people crave, while fame is a great obstacle to completing cultivation. Gradually, this person is bound to become the leader of an evil religion. Because religion's goal is to teach people to be good so that they may eventually return to their heavenly kingdom, the principles it preaches must be higher than those in human society. If they are applied to politics in the human world, this is the most serious corruption of heavenly principles. How can Gods and Buddhas be driven by human attachments and involved in dirty political matters and power struggles in human society? This is what a human being does when driven by his demon-nature. Such a religion is bound to be used by governments to engage in violence and launch religious wars, thereby becoming an evil religion that harms mankind.

Having "all people practice religion" will not do, either. First, this can easily alter religious doctrines and reduce them to theories of ordinary human society. Second, religion can easily be turned into a political tool that will then tarnish the Buddha Fa's image. Third, religious leaders will become politicians, and this will make religion come to an end, thereby turning it into an evil religion.

Falun Dafa is not a religion, but future generations will regard it as one. It is taught to human beings for the purpose of cultivation practice, rather than to establish a religion. There can be a large number of people learning Dafa, but it is not permitted to turn all of a nation's citizens into religious followers and make everyone take part in the unified activities of cultivation practice. Cultivation practice in Dafa is always voluntary. Never force anyone to participate in cultivation practice.

In no period of the future can Dafa be used for any political matters. Dafa can make people's hearts become good, thereby stabilizing society. But by no means is it taught for the purpose of maintaining these things of human society. Disciples, keep in mind that in the future, no matter how much pressure there might be from political and powerful forces, Dafa can never be used by political powers.

Never get involved in politics, nor interfere with state affairs. Genuinely practice cultivation and be good. Keep Dafa pure, unchanged, and indestructible like diamond, and it will thereby exist forever.

Li Hongzhi
September 7, 1996

Further Understanding

On the issue of Buddha-nature and demon-nature, my explanation couldn't have been clearer. As a matter of fact, the tests you have passed were meant for you to remove your demon-nature. Regardless, from time to time you have used various excuses or Dafa to hide it, failing to improve your xinxing and missing the opportunities again and again.

Do you know this? As long as you are a cultivator, in any environment or under any circumstances, any troubles or unpleasant things you come across, even if they involve work for Dafa or no matter how good or sacred you think they are, I will still use them to eliminate your attachments and expose your demon-nature in order to dispose of it since your improvement is the top priority.

If you indeed improve yourselves this way, the things that you do with a pure heart will be the best and most sacred.

Li Hongzhi
September 9, 1996

Cautionary Advice

It has been four years since I began teaching Dafa. Some
practitioners have made very slow progress in xinxing
and level of realm; they remain at the perceptual stage
in their understanding of me and Dafa, always being
grateful towards me for the changes in their bodies and
the manifestation of their supernormal capabilities—
this is an everyday person's understanding. If you do
not want to change the condition of being human and
rationally rise to a genuine understanding of Dafa, you
will miss the opportunity. If you do not change the
human logic that you, as an everyday person, have
formed deep in your bones over thousands of years,
you will not be able to break away from this superficial
human shell and complete cultivation. You cannot
always count on me to eliminate karma for you while
you do not make true progress in the Fa and rise above
human understandings and mentalities. Your ways of
thinking, understanding, and appreciation towards me
and Dafa are the manifestation of everyday people's

thinking. But what I am teaching you is in fact moving beyond everyday people and rationally producing a genuine understanding of Dafa.

In cultivation practice, you are not making real, solid progress on your own, which would make a great fundamental change internally. Instead, you rely on my power and take advantage of powerful external factors. This can never transform your human nature into Buddha-nature. If every one of you can understand the Fa from the bottom of your heart, that will truly be the manifestation of the Fa whose power knows no boundary—the reappearance of the mighty Buddha Fa in the human world!

Li Hongzhi
September 10, 1996

Dafa Can Never be Plagiarized

My disciples! I have been saying repeatedly that imparting Dafa to human beings is already the greatest mercy to them. This is something unprecedented in billions of years! Yet some people simply do not know that they should treasure it. There are others who even want to alter the Fa or the exercises to turn them into something belonging to them, their ethnicity, or their nation. Think about it! You think that it is good because of the self-interest that you are attached to or the interests of your nationality and the like—this is the understanding of everyday people. It would be all right if you were dealing with things of ordinary human society, but this isn't something of everyday people! It is not for your nationality that the Fa is taught. This is the universe's Dafa, the fundamentals of the Buddha Fa! It is imparted to human beings in order to save them. Yet, you have altered such a great Fa...? To alter just a bit of it is already a colossal sin. Be sure never to generate an evil thought simply because of your attachments to ordinary human society! This is extremely dangerous!

Did you know this? In recent years some practitioners suddenly died; some of them died precisely because they did such things. Don't think that your master might do something to you. You should know that there are numerous guardian Gods of the Fa at various levels whose very duty is to protect the Fa. Furthermore, demons won't leave you alone either! It is because you practice cultivation in the upright Fa that you have escaped the karma you owed in your previous lives. Once you are reduced to the level of an everyday person, no one will protect you and demons will also take your life. It is even no use to seek protection with other Buddhas, Taos, and Gods, as they will not protect one who undermines the Fa. Additionally, your karma will also be returned to your body.

It is difficult for one to practice cultivation, yet it is very easy for one to fall. When one fails a test or cannot give up a very strong human attachment, one might reverse himself, taking up the opposite ground. There are too many lessons in history. Only after having fallen down will one begin to regret, yet then it is too late.

Li Hongzhi
September 22, 1996 in Bangkok

What is Enlightenment?

Enlightenment is also called the awakening of wisdom. In our Dafa, it is called kaigong; that is, one has cultivated to completion, finished the entire course of cultivation, and one is about to go to a heavenly kingdom.

Upon awakening, what state will an enlightened being then be in? One who has succeeded in cultivating Buddhahood will become a Buddha; one who has succeeded in cultivating Bodhisattvahood will become a Bodhisattva; one who has succeeded in cultivating Arhatship will become an Arhat; one who cultivates the Tao will attain the Tao; and one who has succeeded in cultivating Godhood will already be a God. Because after completing cultivation some enlightened beings still have something to do in ordinary human society or some wishes to fulfill, they need to live among everyday people for a period of time. But living like this among everyday people is very hard for them. Because they are far too different from everyday people in their realm of thought, they are able to detect clearly all the evil thoughts in the minds of everyday people, such as strong attachments, selfishness, dirtiness, and scheming against others. Also, they can simultaneously detect the slightest mind activities of thousands of people. Furthermore, karma and viruses are everywhere in ordinary human society; there are also many other bad things floating in the air, unknown to human beings. They can see all of these very clearly. Karma in the present-day human society of the Last Havoc is quite enormous. While breathing, people inhale large amounts of karma, viruses, and poisonous gases. It is indeed very difficult for them to stay in this ordinary human world.

So what are they like? This is what those practitioners who are attached to this matter try to figure out. Do not pry into whether he looks like an enlightened one or she looks like one who has completed cultivation. You should put your mind to striving hard in genuine cultivation and also speeding up your completion of cultivation. Why look at others? As a matter of fact, those enlightened people are often disciples who do not show themselves off but engage quietly in genuine cultivation. They are of different ages and look no different from everyday people. It is very likely that they do not attract much attention. Although they possess all the divine powers and abilities of transformation, they find that human beings actually look like tiny, low beings who do not deserve to be shown these things. Moreover, human beings will develop various low-level human understandings and thoughts upon seeing these things, treating them with the human attachment of zealotry; this is intolerable to the enlightened beings. It is difficult for everyday people to understand wherein lies the true significance of the essence of the Buddha Fa divine powers.

At present, some practitioners who care about too many things other than being diligent in cultivation are searching everywhere for enlightened persons and so on. Think about it, everyone: The enlightened ones are already Buddhas and possess everything a Buddha should have. How can they allow people to know them so casually? How can humans know about Buddhas? When you are searching everywhere for them, your attachments, competitiveness, curiosity, mentality of showing off and being meddlesome, combined with the desire of pursuit are at the same time interfering with practitioners' peaceful cultivation practice. Accordingly, do you know how they feel about this? To them, every intentional act or thought of a human being will make them feel uncomfortable!

Because some practitioners have come from very high dimensions to obtain the Fa, they will become enlightened in a very short time. The two-year time for cultivation practice I mentioned was given to these disciples. But all of our Dafa disciples have indeed made very rapid progress in their genuine cultivation; many of them will become enlightened very soon, and this is beyond the imagination of the cultivators in the past. I hope everyone will keep a peaceful mind, making continuous progress with perseverance. As each one completes cultivation, I will receive and deliver each one.

Li Hongzhi
September 26, 1996

Remaking Mankind

The reality known by man is his ignorant understanding of history's development and an illusion created by the empirical sciences. It is not the true manifestation of that great reality within the universe. Furthermore, the genuine reality is bound to bring about a new science and a new understanding. The laws and principles of the universe will appear again in the human world.

Human selfishness, greed, stupidity, and ignorance are interwoven with the goodness inherent in human nature, and humans are unknowingly creating everything they must bear; this is currently swallowing up society. Numerous social problems of various sorts are surfacing in the world and crises lurk everywhere. Yet man does not know to find the cause within his own nature. Unable to see that after the degeneration of morality it is the terrible human heart that is the poisonous root of social problems, man always foolishly tries to find a way out through society's manifestations. As a result, man never realizes that all the so-called "way-outs" he creates for himself are precisely him sealing himself off. As such, there are even fewer way outs, and the new problems that follow will be even worse. Thus, with much difficulty man again finds a tiny space and takes new measures, thereby closing this remaining bit of space once again. As this repeats itself over a period of time, there is no room left and he can no longer find a way out, nor can he see the truth beyond the enclosed space. Man begins to suffer from all that he has created for himself. This is the final way in which the universe eliminates lives.

The Lord of Buddhas, whose mercy is incredibly immense, has left the Buddha Fa to man. The universe is giving man another opportunity, allowing the mighty Buddha Fa once again to reveal the actual reality of the universe to the human world, wash away all filth and ignorance, and use human language to recapture its brilliance and splendor. May you cherish it! The Buddha Fa is right in front of you.

Li Hongzhi
September 28, 1996

Degeneration

The clergy's misconduct completely violates the vows of purity they have taken, makes God's entrustment not worth even a penny, and astonishes both mankind and Gods. Kind-hearted people have been regarding them as the only people whom they can rely on for salvation.

Disappointment has made people increasingly disbelieve in religion, and in the end people have completely lost their faith in God, thereby committing all kinds of bad deeds without any reservations. This has evolved to the extent that people today have completely turned into degenerate people who manifest demonic furor, and this has made all Gods completely lose their confidence in man. This is one of the main reasons why Gods no longer take care of human beings.

Li Hongzhi
October 10, 1996

No Omission in Buddha-Nature

In teaching the Fa, I have mentioned many times that the appearance of scriptures in Sakyamuni's Buddhism and in the Dharma-ending Period was brought about mainly because some people added into the Dharma their own words and understandings—this is the greatest lesson in history. Nevertheless, some disciples simply refuse to abandon their ordinary human attachments. Being taken advantage of by the demon-nature of being attached to showing off their eloquence and literary talents, they unknowingly undermine the Buddha Fa.

Recently, some people have been calling it "dumping dirty water" when practitioners, after deepening their understanding in their cultivation practice, speak of their past shortcomings in sharing their experiences. This has completely changed the content of cultivation practice. Cultivation practice is sacred, and it is not something like an everyday person's self-examination or repentance. Disciples! You should not casually take up a term used or mentioned by everyone. Isn't this adding something human to Dafa? Last year, after the Beijing assistance center put forward the four phrases, I specifically wrote an article, "Correction," for it. It should be taken seriously. Of course, there are still some other improper terms being circulated. You should think about it: If one word is added today and another the day after tomorrow, with the passage of time the next generation of disciples will not be able to tell whose words they are, and gradually Dafa will be changed.

You must be clear that the cultivation practice form that I have left to you can never be altered. Do not do anything that I do not do, and do not use anything that I do not use. In cultivation practice you should say things however I say them. Pay attention! Inadvertent alteration of the Buddha Fa is undermining it all the same!

I also want to tell you that your nature in the past was

94

actually based on egotism and selfishness. From now on, whatever you do, you should consider others first, so as to attain the righteous enlightenment of selflessness and altruism. So from now on, whatever you do or whatever you say, you must consider others—or even future generations—along with Dafa's eternal stability.

Li Hongzhi
February 13, 1997

Sober-Minded

It is time to make a few remarks on the current methods of work employed by assistance center directors in different regions. It is correct to implement the requirements of the Research Society, but you should mind the way you do it. I often say that if all a person wants is the well-being of others and this is without the slightest personal motivation and understanding, what he says will move the listener to tears. I have not only taught you Dafa, but also left you my demeanor. While working, your tone of voice, your kindheartedness, and your reasoning can change a person's heart, whereas commands never can! If others are not convinced in their hearts but only superficially comply, they will still conduct themselves according to their own will when no one is around to see them.

Any work in Dafa is intended for people to obtain the Fa and for disciples to improve themselves. Anything other than these two points is meaningless. Therefore, all activities should be organized according to local conditions and practitioners' situations, instead of being made absolute. Even learning Dafa is voluntary, not to mention organizing activities! As a matter of fact, the person in charge of a center is first of all a leader in studying the Fa. If a person does not study the Fa well himself, he will not do a good job in his work. The experience-sharing conferences organized by assistance centers in different regions should never be turned into self-criticism conferences. Such solemn "Fa Conferences" for sharing cultivation experiences in Dafa should never be turned into exhibitional conferences for exposing the dark side of society, still less should you force practitioners to reveal the shortcomings they had and mistakes they made when they were everyday people; you would thereby inflict serious, negative effects, damaging Dafa's reputation. You should be clear on what you should do and what you should not do. This is solemn cultivation practice. The experience-sharing conferences are intended for the improvement of practitioners and the promotion of Dafa, but not for publicizing how bad our practitioners once were. They are talking about their cultivation practice in Dafa, not dumping so-called "dirty water!" The work you do for Dafa is not irrelevant to your cultivation practice. The factors that improve your xinxing manifest everywhere within your work. You should not only do your work, but also complete cultivation. I know that a few of you seldom read the books or study the Fa, nor do you examine yourselves according to the several articles I have written for you that you call scriptures. What are the "scriptures?" They are simply articles to be read frequently. Do you read them? If you study the Fa more, you will not do a bad job in your work. I point out your shortcomings in order to make Dafa develop in a more healthy way, with fewer problems. In fact, Dafa is also enriching your experience and creating the elite of Dafa.

Li Hongzhi
June 13, 1997 in Hong Kong.

Bear in Mind Forever

Dafa Society:

I suggest that every disciple immediately, on the spot, destroy everything that I have not publicly issued but that are in circulation without permission, such as: my speeches that came out of Chengde; what a practitioner from Beijing said about supernormal capabilities; the speech of the assistance center director in Dalian; the cave story from the director of Guizhou assistance center and other speeches; not to mention the speeches made by people in charge of different regions; what was said by practitioners after seeing me; the speech given by people in charge of the Dafa Research Society, and so on, plus texts, recordings, videotapes, etc., that are transcribed from my speeches without permission. All these must be destroyed on the spot, and they cannot be kept regardless of the excuse. What is "protecting Dafa?" This is most thoroughly a protection of Dafa, and an examination of whether you can follow what I tell you and whether you are truly my disciples! Let me tell everyone once again that the Dharma taught by Buddha Sakyamuni was sabotaged this way. This is a lesson in history. From now on, nobody should tape-record or videotape speeches given by any of the people in charge in different regions or by any disciples; even less can they be edited into texts or be spread around for people to read. This is not a problem of any particular person, nor is this criticizing any person in particular here; instead, this is rectifying Dafa. Bear in mind: except for Dafa practitioners' experience-sharing conferences for studying the Fa and activities organized by major assistance centers with the endorsement of the Research Society, anything that does not belong to Dafa but is being circulated in Dafa undermines Dafa.

Li Hongzhi
June 18, 1997

A Heavy Blow

To make it convenient for more people to practice cultivation, Dafa at present mainly adopts cultivation practice in ordinary human society, and practitioners temper themselves in their workplaces and other ordinary human environments. Only monks and nuns need to roam around. Yet currently some people are traveling around all over the country, calling themselves Dafa disciples. They live in the homes of Dafa disciples for no reason, eating, drinking, taking, and asking for things. Swindling and bluffing, they take advantage of Dafa by capitalizing on the kind nature of practitioners. But why can't our practitioners distinguish them? Cultivation practice is to cultivate one's own self. Think it over. Why don't these people genuinely practice cultivation peacefully in their own homes? A difficult environment can help one cultivate oneself better. Why don't these people listen to my words, moving around all over the country? Why do these people eat, take, and ask for practitioners' things, yet ask them to abandon their attachments? Is this what I've taught them? Even worse, some stay in practitioners' homes for a few months in a row. Isn't this flagrantly interfering with and undermining practitioners' cultivation practice? I think that these people must pay back in full for what they have eaten and taken by swindling. Otherwise, Dafa will not permit it. If such a case occurs again in the future, you can treat that person as a regular swindler and report it to the police, because this person absolutely is not our practitioner.

Also, in some regions people organize the so-called "Fa-preaching groups" without permission, acting pretentiously among practitioners and swindling people everywhere. There are people who also invite individuals to give speeches, thereby undermining and interfering with practitioners' cultivation practice. On the surface these people appear to be promoting Dafa, but in reality they are promoting themselves. A practitioner's cultivation is arranged systematically by my fashen. It is only that some practitioners do not realize this or they are not conscious of it. So aren't these people causing interference? It is especially difficult for those who have just started to learn the Fa to make a clear distinction. There are also people delivering so-called "speeches" in conferences attended by thousands of people. What they have said was all about themselves. They even define some sentences of Dafa or interpret Dafa, with their bodies emitting to the practitioners black karma and the substance of attachments. I have stated explicitly in Zhuan Falun that this is not allowed. Why don't you think it over? Especially for those who are in charge of receptions and inviting people to do such things, you might have inflicted some intangible harm to Dafa disciples, and you are no longer qualified to be in charge of Dafa disciples. Without listening to me or following the requirements of Dafa, how can you be my disciples? Isn't this going against Dafa? If this isn't an undermining of Dafa, then what is it? My disciples, you should not always be unaware of these things until I point them out. In fact, everything is included in the Fa. Why not read the books more? I suggest that everyone set his mind to reading ten times the book I wrote, Essentials for Further Advancement, which you call scripture. When your mind is not at peace, it is no use studying the Fa. You should study it with a peaceful mind.

In a few regions we have people in charge who do not read the books or study the Fa. Furthermore, they claim that they have headaches whenever they read the Fa. Isn't it obvious that demons are interfering with them and yet they don't want to break away from their control? Even a new practitioner can realize this. How can such people be in charge? I think it is better for people like that to voluntarily become common practitioners and genuinely practice cultivation for a period of time peacefully—this is good for both Dafa and themselves. There was also someone who understood my letter of criticism to her in the opposite way and made copies and distributed them to show off, without realizing her mistake, claiming, "Teacher even wrote to me." Also, in order to have practitioners follow their commands, some people in their speeches often use words like, "On behalf of Teacher Li, I ...," and so on. Nobody can represent me. How can your words become my words? What I say is the Fa. Can what you say become the Fa? My disciples! I suggest that you should first become common practitioners for a period of time, and then resume your work after you sober up. No matter how much work a person in charge has done among everyday people, he is working for Dafa out of his own will. The success of his work is only a form of manifestation among everyday people. It is the mighty power of Dafa itself and the specific arrangements made by my fashen that enable people to obtain the Fa and spread the Fa widely. Without my fashen doing these things, even protecting the people in charge can hardly be ensured, let alone spreading the Fa widely. Therefore, do not always think of yourself too highly. There is no fame, self-interest, or official titles in Dafa, but only cultivation practice.

Li Hongzhi
June 18, 1997

Another Comment on Evaluation Criteria

Recently, there have been a great number of new practitioners who have not yet gained a deeper understanding of Dafa's requirements. Especially in some regions, the Dafa practitioners in charge are new, too. Therefore, within a very short time you are required to study the Fa in depth so that all your conduct and demeanor will conform to Dafa. Meanwhile, the general assistance centers in different regions must be careful in selecting people. Those who mislead practitioners should be replaced as soon as possible, and those who study Dafa well should be selected to take charge.

Of late, some assistance centers have asked those whose *tianmu* are purportedly open to examine practitioners' cultivation practice. As a matter of fact, everything those people have seen is a false and illusory. I said long ago that the criterion for evaluating a practitioner was nothing but his xinxing, and I will never allow anyone who has not attained enlightenment or completed cultivation to see clearly the actual situations of my disciples' cultivation practice. What is visible to those who are able to see is merely the manifestation revealed to them at their particular low levels, and they are unable to see things at higher levels. If one who is in charge uses such a person to examine other practitioners, this person will develop a mind for showing off. Moreover, his demon-nature will also cause interference and damage, so what he sees will be transformed by his mind activities. It was wrong for him to examine Dafa disciples in the first place; the person in charge who asked him to examine practitioners also did not follow my words. Why don't you listen to your Master's words: "the only criterion for evaluating a practitioner's cultivation practice is his xinxing?" Don't you know that all dimensions exist simultaneously in the same place? Living beings in any dimension are likely to overlap with human bodies, and they look very much like *futi*. They exist in different dimensions, however, and have nothing to do with humans. Can those whose tianmu are said to be opened understand these complex situations?

Also, some people casually claim that this person has futi or that person has futi. Let me tell everyone that the problem lies in those who make such statements themselves.

The dimensions of the universe are too complex. What I have said thus far has exhausted all expressions of human language. A lot of situations are beyond the description of human language. Even a disciple who has completed cultivation can only see clearly what he has enlightened to at his Fruit Status, not to mention a person who is still practicing cultivation.

Li Hongzhi
June 18, 1997

Definitive Conclusion

Dafa disciples, you must bear in mind that in the future any behavior such as dividing Dafa into units, schools, sects, or denominations, by anyone, at any time, in any place, and with any excuse is undermining the Fa. You should never do what I do not allow you to do. The mind of showing off plus the attachment of zealotry will be most easily exploited by the demonic heart. Whatever you have enlightened to in Dafa is no more than a tiny portion of the Fa's principles at a certain level within the boundless Fa's principles. You must never give definitions for the Fa or a part of it—not even a sentence of it. If you do so in public, the moment you utter it you will have produced sinful karma. In serious cases, the sin can be as big as a mountain or the sky—how could you cultivate yourself? If one alters Dafa and creates another system, his sin will be so great that it is boundless. When a life is paying for that evil karma, the pain from its being eliminated layer after layer will be eternal and endless.

Dafa can rectify the universe, so it certainly has the Fa's power to repress evil, eliminate disorder, harmonize everything, and remain invincible. As a matter of fact, there have been many lessons in this regard. Such affairs of undermining the Fa will be handled by Gods who safeguard the Fa. When all sentient beings treasure Dafa, they are treasuring their own lives and being compassionate to all sentient lives. Dafa is unchangeable and unshakable. It will live on forever and will always exist in the world. Heaven and earth will remain stable forever.

Li Hongzhi
July 1, 1997

A Dialogue with Time

Master: What problems do you find my disciples to still have?

Divine Being: Your disciples can be divided into two groups.

Master: What are the two groups?

Divine Being: One group is able to painstakingly make progress in the Fa by following your requirements. This group is quite good. The other group is attached to human matters, unwilling to give them up, and unable to steadfastly make progress.

Master: Yes, I've seen it.

Divine Being: You gave them a process for understanding the Fa, so some people come with various intentions. After studying the Fa, most of them are able to change their initial purpose for learning the Fa.

Master: Some of them have not changed yet.

Divine Being: Yet it has been too long a time.

Master: Yes!

Divine Being: In my opinion, there is no need to wait for those who cannot become Gods. In fact, they can only be humans.

Master: (talking to himself) In the human world, they are indeed lost too thoroughly. They might have to end up like this. I'm afraid they won't even be qualified to be humans in the end!

Divine Being: Actually it's not bad to become humans in the new world. Compared with those innumerable high-level beings in the universe who have been eliminated by history, they are already incomparably fortunate.

Master: I still want to wait for some time, see what they are like when the more microscopic matter that undermines mankind has been cleaned up, and then make a decision. After all, they have come to obtain the Fa.

Divine Being: At present, in terms of this group of people, some have come to study the Fa because they cannot find their goals in life; they are attached to these notions which they are unwilling to change.

108

Master: There are more such people among new practitioners.

Divine Being: Some of them have come looking for the aspect of the Fa that they consider good, but they are unable to give up the aspect that prevents them from having a complete understanding of the Fa.

Master: There are also such people among veteran disciples. And a most outstanding manifestation is that they always compare themselves with humans and with their own past, but fail to examine themselves with the requirements of the Fa at different levels.

Divine Being: These problems have already become very serious. It would be good if they could manage to search within themselves for the things that they have been able to find in others.

Master: It's time for them to become clear-headed so that their environment can turn into one for genuine cultivation practice, and thus they will be able to become real Gods.

Li Hongzhi
July 3, 1997

Expounding on the Fa

For a long period of time the sentient beings in Dafa, especially the disciples, have had a misunderstanding of the Fa at various levels regarding xinxing improvement. Whenever a tribulation comes, you do not see it with the side of your original nature but view it completely from your human side. Evil demons then take advantage of this point and inflict endless interference and damage, leaving practitioners in long-term tribulations. As a matter of fact, this results from an inadequate understanding of the Fa by your human side. You have humanly restrained your divine side; in other words, you have restrained the parts that have been successfully cultivated and prevented them from rectifying the Fa. How can the uncultivated side restrain your primary thoughts or the side that has already obtained the Fa? Having humanly fostered the evil demons, you allow them to exploit the Fa. When a tribulation arrives, if you, as a disciple, can truly maintain an unshakable calm, or set your mind to meeting different requirements at different levels, this should be sufficient for you to pass the test. If it continues endlessly and if there do not exist other problems in your xinxing or conduct, it must be that the

110

evil demons are exploiting the loopholes caused by your lack of control. After all, a cultivator is not an ordinary person. So why doesn't the side of you that is your original nature rectify the Fa?

There are two reasons why Master did not teach this Fa until today: one is that your problem in this regard has become prominent; the other is that you have gained a very deep understanding of the Fa and will not understand it in a simple way.

You should also be clear that "natural" does not exist, and there is a reason for "inevitability." In fact, "natural" is irresponsibly used by everyday people for self-justification when they are unable to explain the phenomena of the universe, life, and matter. They cannot imagine what "nature" itself is. Under the influence of such a notion you think that all these tribulations are inevitable and this is just the way it is, thereby developing a passive and pessimistic attitude. Therefore, your human side must understand it. More importantly, your side that has obtained the Fa must be clear about it.

Be aware: I am not asking you to do something artificially. I am only trying to make you understand the principles of the Fa so that you will have a clear

111

understanding in this respect. In fact, Dafa is not only to save human beings—it is also taught to all the beings in different dimensions. Your enlightened, original nature will automatically know what to do. Cherishing your human side enables you to ascend in your understanding of the Fa. Dafa is harmonizing all sentient beings, and all sentient beings are also harmonizing Dafa. I have told you the solemnity and sacredness of the Fa in order to eliminate your confusion and misunderstanding of the Fa.

Li Hongzhi
July 5, 1997

Give Up Human Attachments and Continue Genuine Cultivation

With the dissemination of Dafa, more and more people are able to understand Dafa. So we must pay attention to one issue: Do not bring the human concepts of caste and hierarchy into Dafa. Both veteran and new practitioners must be mindful of this issue. Anyone who comes to study the Fa—no matter how learned he is, how big his business, how high he ranks, what special skills he has, or what supernormal capabilities he possesses—must genuinely practice cultivation.

Cultivation practice is magnificent and solemn. Whether you can give up your particular human mindset is a major test that you will have difficulty passing, yet you must pass. After all, as a disciple genuinely practicing cultivation, you must give up this attachment since you can never complete cultivation without abandoning such a mindset.

Veteran practitioners should also pay attention to this issue. As more people study the Fa, you should pay more attention to guiding new practitioners to genuinely practicing cultivation. Meanwhile, you should not relax yourselves. If circumstances permit, you can increase the time spent studying the Fa and practicing the exercises. Maintaining Dafa's tradition, upholding Dafa's cultivation principles, and persevering in genuine cultivation are long-term tests for every Dafa disciple.

Li Hongzhi
July 31, 1997

Take the Middle Way

To have Dafa disciples avoid deviation in their cultivation practice, whenever a common or serious problem appears, I will write an article to point it out in a timely manner so that disciples may realize it and Dafa will suffer fewer losses. This is because whether we can take the right way does not depend only on disciples' righteous cultivation; whether Dafa's overall form is righteous is also a key factor. So, as your teacher, I will often correct the deviations that occur.

Because of disciples' differences in understanding, some disciples always go from one extreme to the other. Whenever they read the Fa I have written they will take extreme actions, thereby causing new problems. When I tell you to change your human understandings, I am not asking you to maintain the human way of understanding Dafa. Yet neither should you be irrational or eccentric. I want you to understand Dafa with a clear mind.

Li Hongzhi
August 3, 1997

The Fa Rectifies the Human Heart

As the number of disciples practicing cultivation in Dafa increases, more and more people want to learn about Dafa. Yet some of them come here not for cultivation practice. Instead, they want to find solutions in Dafa, as they have discovered that there is no way out for human society; this leads to the composition of practitioners as a whole being impure. At the same time, this has also interfered with Dafa from another angle. For instance, some people get some inspiration from Dafa and launch in society something like a civil movement. Such Fa-plagiarizing behavior, which originates from Dafa but fails to validate Dafa, counteracts Dafa from another perspective. As a matter of fact, no movement can bring about a fundamental change in the human mind. Nor will their phenomena last—as time goes on, people will become indifferent. Afterwards, there will emerge unhealthy phenomena that are harder to tackle. Dafa absolutely can not fall into such a state.

At present, of all the good citizens and good deeds publicized by the media—such as radio, TV, newspapers, etc., many have been done by our Dafa practitioners since they practice cultivation in Dafa and have improved their xinxing. The news reports, however, claim that these people have done so because they are role models or backbone figures, etc., thereby completely disregarding the fact that their conduct was a result of their cultivation practice in Dafa. This is mainly caused by disciples themselves. Cultivation practice is a great and magnificent matter. Why can't you tell the interviewers in an open and dignified manner that you do those things because you practice cultivation in Dafa? If the reporter does not want to mention Dafa, we should not gloss over any form that plagiarizes Dafa but fails to validate it. All of us are trying to be good people, and this is in the interest of society and mankind. Why can't we have a fair and legitimate environment? Disciples, you should bear in mind that Dafa is perfecting you and you are also fulfilling Dafa.

Li Hongzhi
August 17, 1997

Principles for Disciples Who Are Monks and Nuns

Recently, a number of disciples who are monks and nuns in a religion have begun practicing cultivation in Dafa. To enable themselves to improve as quickly as possible, they should give up the bad habits modern religions have developed over a long period of time. In this regard, our Dafa disciples practicing cultivation among everyday people should not encourage them to develop such things. The cultivation method that Buddha Sakyamuni left for monks and nuns was very good. But modern monks and nuns have altered it because many of them cannot let go of their attachments to money. They have even made up some excuses to justify themselves over this, such as renovating temples, building Buddha statues, printing Buddhist scriptures, covering the expenses for maintaining temples, and so on. None of these are cultivation practice; instead, they are all purposeful actions that have nothing to do with genuine cultivation, and one absolutely cannot complete cultivation by means of them.

To practice cultivation in Dafa one must give up attachments to money and possessions. Otherwise, how can one meet the standard for being a Dafa disciple? Additionally, except in special situations, disciples who are monks and nuns are not allowed to travel by motor vehicle, plane, or ship. All should travel on foot. Only through enduring hardships can one repay one's karma. When hungry, one can collect alms with an alms-bowl (one should only beg for food, but never for money or goods). At night, one may stay at the homes of Dafa disciples in different regions, but not for long. You must set strict requirements for yourselves! Otherwise, you are not my disciples. Because disciples who are monks and nuns have different cultivation circumstances from those of disciples who practice cultivation at home, society does not treat you as everyday people, either. To complete cultivation soon, disciples who are monks and nuns should temper themselves in the human world. You should never be attached to comfort or pleasure, nor should you use any excuse to seek fame or gain. Still less should you ask for money to send home. If you cannot give up worldly thoughts, you should not have become a monk or nun. In ancient times there were very strict requirements for becoming a monk or nun. Dafa disciples who are monks and nuns should set even stricter requirements for themselves. Since you have become a monk or nun, why can't you let go of worldly thoughts?

Disciples! As for disciples practicing cultivation at home, they will gradually, thoroughly abandon attachments to the secular world. But for disciples who are monks and nuns, it is a prerequisite that they must meet from the very beginning as well as a standard for becoming a monk or nun.

Li Hongzhi
October 16, 1997

Environment

The cultivation practice form that I have left for Dafa disciples ensures that disciples can truly improve themselves. For example, I ask you to practice the exercises as a group in parks to form an environment.

This environment is the best way to change the surface of a person. The lofty conduct that Dafa disciples have established in this environment—including every word and every act—can make people realize their own weaknesses and identify their shortcomings; it can move one's heart, refine one's conduct, and enable one to make progress more rapidly. Therefore, new practitioners or self-taught disciples must go to the exercise sites to do the exercises. There are currently about 40 million practitioners in China participating daily in group practice at the exercise sites; there are tens of millions of veteran disciples who do not go to the exercise sites very often (for veteran disciples, this is normal, as this results from their state in cultivation practice). Nevertheless, as new disciples you should never miss such an environment. This is because all of those whom you come into contact with in society are everyday people. Furthermore, they are everyday people who have undergone a rapid decline in human morality. In this big dye vat, people can only drift along with the current.

There are also many new Dafa practitioners who are secretly practicing at home, fearing the embarrassment of others finding out. Think about it: What kind of thought is this? An ordinary fear is an attachment that needs to be eliminated through cultivation practice. Yet you are afraid of others finding out that you are learning

119

Dafa? Cultivation practice is a very serious matter. How should you treat yourself and the Fa? There are also some people in leadership positions that find it embarrassing to go out and practice the exercises. If you cannot even overcome such a trivial feeling, what can you cultivate? In fact, even if you go to the exercise site, there might not be people who know you. In some workplaces, almost all the executives are learning Dafa, but no one knows that the others are also learning. The environment is created by you, yourselves, and it, too, is essential for your improvement. I often find that you are in a good state of mind when you study the Fa or do the exercises, but when you come into contact with your work and other people, you become the same as everyday people. You sometimes appear even worse than everyday people. How can this be the conduct of a Dafa disciple?

I want to treat you as my disciples, but what should I do if you, yourselves don't want to be my disciples? Every attachment for you to remove in your cultivation practice is a wall, standing there and blocking your path of cultivation practice. If you are unable to be determined about the Fa itself, you cannot practice cultivation. Do not take your position among everyday people too seriously. Do not think that others will fail to understand you if you learn Dafa. Think about it: Even man's claim

that he has evolved from apes can be highly regarded.
Yet even with such a great Dafa of the universe, you are
embarrassed to give it a correct position—this is man's
true shame.

Li Hongzhi
October 17, 1997

Digging Out the Roots

Recently, a few scoundrels from the literary, scientific,
and qigong communities, who have been hoping to
achieve fame through opposing qigong, have been
constantly causing trouble, as though the last thing they
want to see is a peaceful world. Some newspapers, radio
stations and TV stations in various parts of the country
have directly resorted to these propaganda tools to
undermine our Dafa, having a very bad impact on the
public. These are deliberate underminings of Dafa and
cannot be ignored. Under such very special
circumstances, Dafa disciples in Beijing adopted a
special approach to ask those people to stop undermining
Dafa—this actually was not wrong. This is only done
in extremely restricted situations (other regions should
not copy their approach). But when practitioners
voluntarily approach those uninformed and irresponsible

media agencies and explain to them our true situation, this should not be considered wrong.

What I would like to tell you is not whether this incident itself was right or wrong. Instead, I want to point out that such an event has exposed some people. They still have not fundamentally changed their human mindset, and they still perceive problems with the human mentality wherein human beings protect human beings. I have said that Dafa absolutely should not get involved in politics. The purpose of this event itself was to help the media understand our actual situation and learn about us positively so that they would not drag us into politics. Speaking from another perspective, Dafa can teach the human heart to be good and it can stabilize society. But you must be clear that Dafa certainly is not taught for these purposes, but rather for cultivation practice.

Dafa has created a way of existence for mankind at the lowest level. Then, among various human behaviors within the human form of existence at this level, including collectively presenting actual facts to someone, etc., isn't this one of the numerous forms of existence that Dafa gives to mankind at the lowest level? It is just that when people do things, good and evil coexist. Thus, there will be struggles and politics. Under extremely special circumstances, however, Dafa disciples adopted such an approach from the Fa at the lowest level, and they completely applied their kind side. Wasn't this an act that harmonized the Fa at the level of mankind? Except under special extreme circumstances, such an approach is not to be adopted.

I have long noticed that a few individuals do not have the heart to protect Dafa, but instead intend to protect certain things in human society. If you were an everyday person I would have no objection; it is certainly a good thing to be a good person who protects human society. But now you are a cultivator. What standpoint you take in treating Dafa is a fundamental issue; it is also precisely what I want to point out to you. During your cultivation practice, I will use every means to expose all of your attachments and dig them out at the root.

You cannot always rely on me to bring you up to a higher level while you, yourself do not move. Only after the Fa is explicitly stated do you make a move. If it is not taught clearly, you do not move, or move backward. I cannot recognize such behavior as cultivation practice. At the crucial moment when I ask you to break away from humans, you do not follow me. Each opportunity will not occur again. Cultivation practice is a serious matter. The distance has become greater and greater. It is extremely dangerous to add anything human to cultivation practice. In fact, it is also fine to just be a good person. But you must be clear that you choose your own path.

Through this event, it has been observed that several individuals ran around among disciples causing damage. Instead of thinking correctly and presenting their views kindly to the assistance centers, they spread rumors among practitioners, sowed discord, organized factions, and adopted the worst methods of everyday people. Furthermore, some people even irrationally tried to drive practitioners away. Some of the practitioners whom you tried to drive away have cultivated themselves many times better than you have. Have you thought about this? Why did you act so irrational and resentful? Even with such a mentality could you still not recognize your strong attachment? Let me tell everyone: This Fa is inconceivably enormous, and you will never completely know or understand its laws and principles.

I do not care for formalities. I will use various means to expose your deeply-concealed attachments and get rid of them.

Li Hongzhi
July 6, 1998

For Whom do You Exist?

The most difficult things for people to give up are their
notions. Some people cannot change—even if they have
to give up their lives for false doctrines. Yet such notions
are themselves acquired postnatally. Man always
believes that such unshakable ideas—ideas which can
make him pay any price without a second thought—are
his own thoughts. Even when he sees the truth he will
reject it. In fact, other than one's innate purity and
innocence, all notions are acquired postnatally and are
not one's actual self.

If these acquired notions become very strong, they will
reverse their role and dictate one's real thinking and
behavior. At this point, a person may still think that
they are his own ideas. This is the case for almost all
contemporary people.

In dealing with relevant, important issues, if a life can
really, without any preconceptions, assess issues, then
this person is truly able to take charge of himself. Such
soberness is wisdom, and it is different from average
people's so-called "intelligence." If a person cannot do
that, then he is dictated by acquired notions or external
thoughts. He may even devote his entire life to

struggling for them; but when he gets old, he will not even know what he has been doing this lifetime. Though he has achieved nothing in his lifetime, he has committed innumerable mistakes while being driven by these acquired notions. Therefore, in his next life he must pay for the karma according to his own wrong deeds.

When a person becomes agitated, what controls his thoughts and feelings is not reason, but emotion. When a person's various notions, such as his faith in science, religion, or an ideology, etc., are being challenged by the truth of the Buddha Fa, he will also become agitated. This causes the evil side of human nature to predominate, thereby making him become even more irrational; it is a result of being controlled by the acquired notions. He will blindly jump to conclusions or complicate the matter. Even a person with a predestined relationship can lose this preordained opportunity because of this, turning his own actions into eternal, deep regrets.

Li Hongzhi
July 11, 1998

Dissolving Into the Fa

At present, more and more people are becoming Dafa practitioners, and there is a trend wherein newcomers have a better perceptual understanding. With no obstacles from the ultra-leftist thinking that earlier existed in society, or from conceptual processes of understanding, they do not need to spend a great amount of time on discussion during group study of the Fa. So they should spend a great amount of time studying the Fa to elevate themselves as quickly as possible. The more your mind holds, the faster the change.

I once talked about what is a good person and what is a bad person. It is not that one who appears to have committed a bad deed is a bad person and one who has done something good is a good person. Some people's minds are full of bad thoughts—it is only that they have not shown them or have slyly concealed them relatively well; yet these are truly bad people. Some people, on the other hand, are not bad to begin with but occasionally commit wrong deeds; these people are not necessarily bad people. Then how should we understand good people and bad people?

A person is like a container: he is whatever he contains. All of what a person sees with the eyes and hears with the ears are: violence, lust, power struggles in literary works, struggles for profit, worship of money, other manifestations of demon-nature, and so on, of the practical world. With his head filled with these, such a person is truly a bad person, no matter what he appears to be. One's behavior is dictated by one's thoughts. With a mind full of such things, what's one able to do? It is only because everyone's mind is more or less contaminated to some extent that people cannot detect the problem that has surfaced. Incorrect social trends that are reflected in every aspect of society are imperceptibly changing people, poisoning mankind, and creating a large number of so-called "anti-tradition," "anti-upright," and "anti-moral" human beings with demon-nature. This is what's truly worrisome! Even though society's economy has made progress, it will be ruined in these people's hands since they do not have human ways of thinking.

On the contrary, if a person accepts the kind, traditional thoughts of mankind that have prevailed for thousands of years, believes in proper human behavior and standards, and is filled with all good things, what will this person's conduct be like? Whether or not this person shows it, he is a genuinely good person.

As a practitioner, if his mind is filled with nothing but

128

Dafa, this person is definitely a genuine cultivator. So you must have a clear understanding on the issue of studying the Fa. Reading the books more and studying the books more is the key to genuinely upgrading yourself. To put it more simply, as long as you read Dafa, you are changing; as long as you read Dafa, you are elevating. The boundless content of Dafa plus the supplementary means—the exercises—will enable you to complete cultivation. Group reading or reading by yourself is the same.

The ancients have a saying, "Having heard the Tao in the morning, one can die in the evening." No one in mankind today can really understand its meaning. Do you know that when a person's mind accepts the Fa, isn't that part of his mind that accepts the Fa assimilated to the Fa? Where will that part go upon the death of the person who has heard the Fa? I ask you to study the Fa more, remove more attachments, and give up various human notions, so that you will not take away with you only a certain part, but reach completion.

Li Hongzhi
August 3, 1998

The Buddha Fa and Buddhism

Many people think of Buddhism whenever Buddha is mentioned. Actually, Buddhism is only one form of the Buddha Fa's manifestations in the human world. The Buddha Fa manifests itself in other ways as well as in the human world. In other words, Buddhism cannot represent the entire Buddha Fa.

As for Buddhism, not everything in it was taught by Buddha Sakyamuni. There are other forms of Buddhism in the world that do not revere Buddha Sakyamuni as their master. In fact, some have nothing to do with Buddha Sakyamuni. For example, what the Yellow Sect of Tibetan Buddhism worships is the Great Sun Tathagata, and it regards Buddha Sakyamuni as a Buddha fashen of the Great Sun Tathagata. With Milerepa as its object of worship, the White Sect of Tibetan Buddhism has nothing to do with Buddha Sakyamuni, nor does it mention Sakyamuni's Buddhism. Their believers during that time did not even know the name of Buddha Sakyamuni, let alone who Buddha Sakyamuni was. Other sects of Tibetan Buddhism have each understood Buddha Sakyamuni differently. Theravada has always regarded itself as the orthodox Buddhism taught by Buddha Sakyamuni, for it has indeed inherited, in formality, the cultivation method used in the era of Buddha Sakyamuni. It has kept the original precepts and dress, and it worships only Buddha Sakyamuni. Chinese Buddhism was altered before it was introduced into China. The cultivation method was changed drastically, with the worship of many Buddhas instead of Buddha Sakyamuni alone. In the meantime, the precepts have doubled in number and the rites of ancient China's civil religions have been incorporated. During religious ceremonies, Chinese musical instruments—such as wooden fish, bells, gongs and drums—are used, and ancient civilian clothes are worn. It was renamed "Mahayana," and has become considerably different from Buddha Sakyamuni's early Buddhism. Therefore, Theravada at that time did not recognize Mahayana as Sakyamuni's Buddhism.

The above has been mentioned to address the relationship between the Buddha Fa and Buddhism in the context of Buddhism. Now let me discuss it from a historical perspective. In Western society, among the unearthed relics of ancient Greek culture, the svastikam emblem has been discovered. In fact, in the remote ages before Noah's Flood, Buddha was also worshipped. At the time of the Flood, some people of ancient Greek ancestry living in western Asia and the region to the southwest of the Himalayas survived. They were then called "Brahman," and they became today's white Indians. As a matter of fact, Brahmanism worshipped Buddha initially. It had inherited the tradition of revering Buddha from the ancient Greeks who, at that time, called Buddha "God." About a thousand years later, Brahmanism began its transfiguration, just like the alterations of Buddhism in modern Mahayana, the alterations in Tibetan Buddhism, the alterations in Japanese Buddhism, and so on. Over a thousand years later in ancient India, Brahmanism began its Dharma-ending period. People started to worship messed up objects rather than Buddha. At that time Brahman people no longer believed in Buddha. Instead, what they worshipped were all demons. Killing and sacrificing animals as ritual worship took place. By the time Buddha Sakyamuni was born, Brahmanism had already become a completely evil religion. This is not to say that Buddha had changed, but that the religion had become evil. Among the remaining cultural relics from ancient India, one can still find statues left by early Brahmanism in the mountain caves. The carved statues of Gods all resemble the image of Buddha. They can also be found in Buddhism among the Buddha sculptures in China. For instance, in several major caves there are statues of two seated Buddhas facing each other, etc. The Buddha was still Buddha—it was the religion that had become evil. Religion does not represent Gods or Buddha. It was the deterioration of the human mind that deformed the religion.

All of this shows that the Buddha Fa is eternal and that the Buddha Fa is the nature of the universe. It is the mighty Buddha Fa that created Buddhas, and not Buddha Sakyamuni that created the Buddha Fa. Buddha Sakyamuni was enlightened to the Buddha Fa, enlightening up to the level of his fruit status.

Let me make a few more remarks in terms of this cycle of human civilization. Do you know that Tao is one kind of God; Buddha is another kind of God; Jehovah, Jesus, and St. Mary are also one kind of God? Their fruit status and bodily forms vary as a result of differences in their cultivation objectives and in their understandings of the universe's Dafa. It is the Buddha Fa that created the immense cosmic body, and not these Buddhas, Taos, and Gods. This much is known to human beings. How much more remains unknown to mankind is still enormous! Didn't Buddha Sakyamuni once say that with respect to Tathagata Buddhas alone, they are as many as the grains of sand in the river Ganges? Could the teachings by these Buddhas be the same as the Dharma expounded by Buddha Sakyamuni? Could the teachings they would give, if and when they came to human society, match the Dharma taught by Buddha

Sakyamuni word for word? Had the seven Buddhas before Buddha Sakyamuni taught the Dharma Buddha Sakyamuni taught? It is mentioned in Buddhism that the future Buddha, Buddha Maitreya, will come to this human world to preach his teachings. Will he then repeat Buddha Sakyamuni's words? I feel sad to find Buddhism today having reached such a stage, being foolishly obsessed with religion itself rather than genuinely practicing cultivation. Hypocrites and religious rogues are seriously corrupting the cultivation places and monks. On second thought, it is not so surprising. As a matter of fact, Buddha Sakyamuni once talked about the conditions of the Dharma-ending period. To what extent does modern Buddhism differ from Brahmanism in its later period?

At present, I have once again come to this world to teach the Fa and to directly teach the fundamental law of the universe. Some people do not dare to admit this fact—not because they are concerned about their own cultivation, but rather for the purpose of protecting religion itself or because they allow their ordinary people's sentiments to get in the way. They equate religion with Buddha. There are others who object, using their ordinary human minds, because their prominence in Buddhism is challenged. Is this a small attachment? As for those with ulterior motives who dare to even slander the Buddha Fa and Buddhas, they have already become ghosts in hell. It is just that their lives on earth are not over yet. They always consider themselves to be some sort of religious scholars. Yet how much do they really know about the Buddha Fa! Oftentimes, as soon as Buddha is mentioned, they will immediately relate it to Buddhism; as soon as the Buddha School is mentioned, they will think that it is the Buddhism of their denomination; as soon as the Buddha Fa is mentioned, they will regard it as what they know. There are many people around the world who practice cultivation deep in the mountains for a long time. Many of them practice cultivation by following different cultivation ways in the Buddha School that have been passed down for hundreds of years. They have nothing to do with Sakyamuni's religion. For those religious rogues who are not even clear about these concepts or terms, what kind of qualifications do they have to criticize Falun Dafa? In the past, Jesus's appearance upset Judaism. Two thousand five hundred years ago, Sakyamuni's appearance shook Brahmanism. It seems that people can never learn positive lessons from history. Instead, they always learn from negative lessons for the sake of their own self-interests. In the universe, there is the law of formation, settlement, and deterioration. Nothing is constant without change. There are Buddhas in different historical periods who come to this world to save people. History develops in this way. Mankind in the future will also hear of the Buddha Fa.

Li Hongzhi
December 17, 1998

Dafa Cannot be Exploited

Dafa can save all beings. Standing before the great facts, even those so-called "high-level beings" who are escaping into the Three Realms and those from the Three Realms who have done damage to Dafa can no longer deny it. Nevertheless, a problem has come along and manifested itself among everyday people. For example, some people who used to oppose Dafa or did not believe in Dafa have also come to learn to practice Dafa. Dafa can save all beings. I do not object to anyone coming to learn it, and in fact I have been teaching Dafa to all beings. The key point is that in their hearts these people do not regard me as their genuine master. Their purpose for learning Dafa is to use it to protect in their hearts things that they cannot give up, things in religion, or God. This is an act of plagiarizing the Fa. The intention of taking advantage of Dafa is itself an unforgivable sin. For some of them, however, the human side of their mind is not quite so clear; therefore, I have been observing them all along. Because I think that, regardless of the reason they have taken the path of Dafa, it is still a rare opportunity for them—I am giving wrongdoers another chance. After all, he or she was born into a time when Dafa is being spread widely, and he or she is also in a human body. I have been waiting for them to come to realize this.

As a matter of fact, there is also a group of people who came like this and have completely changed their original perception, becoming determined and genuine Dafa disciples. But there is still another group of people who do not intend to change and who have long been stumbling along in Dafa. For the sake of Dafa's stability in the human world, I cannot condone their continuing any further. Thus, they will really miss their chance. As I said, superficial changes are for others to see. Whether or not you can be saved depends on the change and transcendence of your own heart. If change does not occur there, one will not be able to improve and nothing can be achieved. Actually, it is because of reading <u>Zhuan Falun</u> that your body has been somewhat blessed on the surface. Other than that, you have not attained anything. With such an ill mind, can you attain anything else? Human beings! Think about it! What should you believe? What shouldn't you believe? Why do you practice cultivation? For whom do you practice cultivation? For whom does your life exist? I trust that you will weigh such questions properly. Otherwise, what you will lose can never be made up. When Dafa manifests itself to mankind, these are not the only things that you will lose.

Li Hongzhi
March 16, 1999

Determination and Solidity

The Buddha Fa cultivation practice is majestic. At the same time, it is also serious. Disciples, you only know that there exist truth and falsehood in the secular world, but you do not know that lives in other dimensions— including Gods—vary greatly in the universe, due to their different levels. This leads to differences in their understandings of matters and the truth. In particular, due to the circumstance that they are unclear about the reality regarding the rectification of the Fa, some have caused severe interference and resistance, inflicting damage by using different methods to come into contact with students. They have thereby caused some practitioners whose tianmu are opened at low levels to have doubts and confusion about Dafa. Among these beings within the Three Realms (the so-called "deities") and the various so-called "high-level beings" who have fled over from higher dimensions in order to escape the rectification with the Fa, most of them do not know the truth regarding the rectification of the Fa and resist the rectification of the Fa itself. They are undermining the students' upstanding faith and determination by exhibiting or telling the practitioners some of their understandings based on their own notions, or by imparting some things to the students, and so on. Actually, those are all very low-level things and deceptive lies. As they are Gods, they appear to be very kind, causing a group of students who have insufficient understanding of Dafa to develop wavering thoughts. Consequently, some people have stopped studying Dafa, and some have even taken up the opposite side. At present, this problem is very serious. Because of this, these people's situation is extremely lamentable. At the same time, what they have lost will never be regained, and this is a major calamity in their lives.

I have already mentioned all of this to you in <u>Essentials for Further Advancement</u> and in <u>Zhuan Falun,</u> in the topics: "no second cultivation way," and how to practice cultivation with tianmu open. Why can't you handle yourself properly once you see those hypocritical, so-called "higher beings" talking to you? Can they have you complete cultivation? Why don't you think about it? Why did they ignore you before you learned Dafa? Why do they become so concerned about you after you have learned Dafa? Cultivation practice is a serious matter. I have already taught you all the principles of the Fa. All of these are things that you have to go through and tests that you have to pass in your personal cultivation practice. Failing to pass them is your own doing. All this time I have been giving you opportunities to realize it and to get back on track. For the sake of Dafa, I cannot wait any longer and have to write this article. I know that when you read this article you will be bound to be awakened; but this does not come from your own cultivation. Why haven't others been interfered with? I have said that the rectification of the Fa started from outside of the Three Realms, and therefore some so-called "deities" within the Three Realms could not see it. Thus, they dared to do things that undermine Dafa. When the rectification of the Fa entered the Three Realms and the human world, they had nowhere to escape to. Moreover, there are records of everything they have done which, then, become the future positions that they place themselves into. Some will lower their levels, and some will become human beings. Some will become ghosts in the nether world, and some will be completely destroyed through almost endless and repeated destruction as payment for all that they have done; this is because those are the positions they get through the most truthful exhibition of their own xinxing. This way, all lives from above are also rearranging their positions in Dafa, not to mention these things in the human world and its everyday people. In the rectification of the Fa, there are those who ascend, there are those who descend, and there are those who are destroyed. Regardless of whether they are Gods, human beings, or ghosts, all will be placed anew in each position of different realms—from survival to total elimination. You human beings are treasured because you are able to practice cultivation; that is why you are taught principles of such high levels. You are treasured because through cultivation you are capable of becoming truly great enlightened beings with virtuous enlightenment and righteous Fa.

Li Hongzhi
March 16, 1999

Purging Demon-Nature

In the wake of the Western U.S. Dafa Experience Sharing Conference, some people who listened to the Fa with attachments claimed that cultivation practice would soon come to an end and that Master would leave, taking some practitioners with him. This is an act that seriously damages Dafa, and it is a massive exposure of demon-nature. When did I ever make such statements? This is the result of your wild imagination energized by your attachments. How do you know that you will complete cultivation? How can you complete cultivation when you are even unable to give up your personal attachments? Dafa is serious. How can it follow what evil religions do? What other forms of demon-nature do you still harbor? Why do you have to switch to the opposite side of Dafa? If you still want to be my disciples, immediately stop being used by demons when you are talking.

Disciples, I have said repeatedly that cultivation practice is both serious and sacred. At the same time, our cultivation practice should be responsible to society, mankind, and ourselves. Why can't you practice cultivation honorably and in a way that conforms to ordinary human society? For all those who told others that there was no time left, that they were making their final arrangements, or that the Master would leave and take so-and-so with him, and so on, I suggest that you immediately undo the impact that you have either directly or indirectly caused. Not even one sentence should be taken advantage of by demons. Our way of completing cultivation must be aboveboard.

Li Hongzhi
March 30, 1999

True Nature Revealed

Firmly cultivate Dafa with the heart unmoved,
The improvement of one's level is fundamental,
In the face of trials, one's true nature is revealed,
Complete cultivation, becoming a Buddha, Tao or God.

Li Hongzhi
May 8, 1999

Some Thoughts of Mine

Recently it was reported in the news that Mainland
China seeks a reduction of US$500 million worth of
trade surplus (with the U.S.) in exchange for my
extradition back to China. With regard to this issue, I
would like to make some comments. I only teach people
to be compassionate. At the same time, I unconditionally
help people eliminate their illnesses, and I enable them
to reach higher realms of mind. I do not accept any
monetary or material reward. All of these have had a
positive impact on society and mankind, bringing

143

goodness to people's hearts and dignity to human morality. Are those the reasons for which they seek my extradition? Do they intend to have me return to China to let more people obtain the Fa and cultivate their hearts? If that is the case, please do not let the country lose US$500 million to strike a deal. I can go back myself.

I have heard, however, that normally the people who are extradited are all war criminals, public enemies, or criminal offenders. If so, I do not know into which of the above categories I would be placed.

As a matter of fact, I keep teaching people to conduct themselves according to the guiding principles of Zhen-Shan-Ren. So naturally I have also been setting an example. During the times when Falun Gong disciples and I, myself were being discredited for no reason and being treated unfairly, we always exhibited hearts of great compassion and tolerance so as to give the government sufficient time to understand us, and we endured all of it silently. Nevertheless, such endurance absolutely is not because Falun Gong practitioners and I fear anything. It should be known that once a person learns the truth and the genuine meaning of life's existence, he will not regret giving up his life for that. Do not take our hearts of compassion and great tolerance as fear, so as to double the efforts [against us] recklessly. In fact, those are enlightened practitioners, and they are cultivators who have learned the genuine meaning of life. Also, do not label Falun Gong practitioners as people who engage in alleged "superstition." There are so many things that mankind and science have not yet come to understand. As far as religions are concerned, don't they also exist as a result of faith in God(s)? In reality, it is only the true religions and ancient beliefs in God(s) that have enabled the morality of human society to be maintained for several thousand years, making the existence of today's mankind—which includes you, me, him, etc.—possible. If this were not the case, mankind would have committed sins long ago that led to disasters. Human ancestors probably would have become extinct long ago, and today's events would never have occurred. Human morality is, in fact, extremely important. If people do not value virtue, they can commit all kinds of wrongdoing that are extremely dangerous to mankind. This is what I can tell people. Actually, I have no intention of doing anything for society, nor do I wish to get involved in issues of everyday people at all, let alone take power away from anybody. Not everyone considers power to be so important. Isn't there a saying among mankind that "everyone has his own will"? I only wish to let those who can practice cultivation obtain the Fa, as well as teach them how to genuinely improve xinxing; that is, to elevate their moral standards. Furthermore, not everyone will come to learn Falun Gong. Also, what I am doing is bound to have no relationship with politics. Yet, for any country or nationality it is a good thing to have cultivators whose hearts have embraced benevolence and whose moral levels have been upgraded. How can it be labeled an evil religion for helping people to heal their sicknesses and keep fit, while raising human moral standards? Every Falun Gong practitioner is a member of society, and each has his own job and career. They simply go to the parks to practice Falun Gong exercises for half an hour or an hour every morning, then going off to work. There are no required religious regulations of any kind to observe, nor are there any temples, churches, or religious rituals. People can come to learn it or leave as they please— there is no binding membership. In what way does it have anything to do with religion? As to the label "evil," how can it fall into the category of "evil" for teaching people to be benevolent, healing people's sicknesses, and keeping them fit without accepting any money [from them]? Or should something be considered evil if it is outside the category of communist theories? Besides, I know, evil religion is just evil religion, and it is not up to a government to decide. Should an evil religion be called "upright" if it conforms to the views of some people in government? On the other hand, should an upright one be defined as evil if it does not conform to their views?

Actually, I know exactly why some people insist on opposing Falun Gong. Just as reported by the media, there are too many people practicing Falun Gong. A hundred million people is indeed no small number. Yet why should having too many good people be feared? Isn't it true that the more good people there are, the better, while the fewer bad people there are, the better? I, Li Hongzhi, unconditionally help practitioners improve their moral quality and keep people healthy, and this in turn stabilizes society. Additionally, with their healthy bodies, people can better serve society. Isn't this bringing good fortune to the people in power? In reality, this has indeed been achieved. Why, instead of recognizing this and showing me appreciation, do they want to estrange more than 100 million people from the government? What kind of government would be so inconceivable? Furthermore, among these 100 million people, who doesn't have a family and children, relatives and friends? Is it merely an issue of 100 million people? So the number of the people they are going against could be even more. What has actually happened to "the leadership of my beloved country"? If I, with the life of Li Hongzhi, can dispel the fears towards these good people, I will go back at once and leave everything to their disposal. Why bother with "going against the will of the law under heaven," wasting manpower and capital, and using politics and money to seek a deal that violates human rights? The United States, however, has been a leader in respecting human rights. Given this, how could the U.S. government be willing to betray human rights for such a deal? In addition, I am a U.S. permanent resident that lives under the jurisdiction of U.S. law.

I do not intend to condemn any particular person. It is just that I do not understand the way things are being handled. Why miss a good opportunity to appeal to the hearts of the people, instead placing more than 100 million people on the opposing side?

It was reported that many people went to Zhongnanhai and that some people were outraged by this. In fact, the number of people who went there was not large at all. Think about it, everyone: There are over 100 million people practicing Falun Gong, and only over ten thousand people showed up. How can that be considered a large number? There was no need to mobilize practitioners. Among 100 million practitioners, since you wanted to go and he wanted to go, in a short while, over ten thousand people would be there. They did not have any slogans or any signs, nor was there any improper conduct. Furthermore, they were not against the government. They merely wished to present the facts to the government. What was wrong with that? Please allow me to ask: Have there ever been such well-behaved demonstrators? Shouldn't one be moved by such a sight? Why do some people keep trying to find fault with Falun Gong? Besides, the approach of resorting to any and all means in order to eliminate Falun Gong is really outdated. Falun Gong is not terrible, as some people might have imagined it to be. Instead, it is a great thing. Any society has everything to gain from it and nothing to lose. On the contrary, losing the hearts of people is the most formidable thing. To be frank, the practitioners of Falun Gong are also human beings who are in the process of practicing cultivation; so they still have human minds. As they are being treated unjustly, I am not sure how much longer they will be able to endure it. This is the issue about which I am most concerned.

Li Hongzhi
June 2, 1999

Position

The trials that a practitioner goes through are trials that everyday people cannot bear. Therefore, those in history who were able to succeed in cultivation and achieve completion are few and far between. Human beings are just human beings. On critical occasions it is very hard for them to give up their human thinking, and they always find excuses to convince themselves. In the midst of crucial tests, however, a great cultivator is able to give up his ego and all of his ordinary human thinking. I congratulate those Dafa cultivators who have made it through the tests that determine whether they can complete cultivation. The eternity in which your lives are unending and the level where you will be in the future—these you establish yourselves. Mighty virtues are cultivated by you, yourselves. So strive forward. This is the greatest and the most magnificent thing.

Li Hongzhi
June 13, 1999

Stability

With regard to the events that occurred a short time ago, they have already caused many Falun Dafa practitioners serious harm. At the same time, they have also severely tarnished the nation's image. Based on what they know regarding how the relevant regions or the relevant departments directly or covertly interfered with and disrupted the practice sessions of Falun Gong students, students can report these cases through the usual channels to the various levels of the government or the country's leadership. As for the situation whereby some people used the power that they held to instigate the Falun Gong incident—putting a broad segment of the people and government in opposition to each other as an opportunity to seize political capital—this may also be reported through the usual channels to the various levels of the government or the country's leadership.

We are cultivators, however. Do not participate in politics and do not be disturbed by these previous events. Calm your hearts, resume your normal practice, study the Fa, strive forward, and cultivate solidly, constantly improving yourselves.

Li Hongzhi
June 13, 1999

Further Comments on Superstition

Initially, "superstition" was just an ordinary term. Some people in political circles in China hyped it into a term with deadly power. Actually, superstition as publicized by those in political circles is not superstition, but a political label and a political slogan; it is a political term used specifically when attacking others. Once something is slapped with this label, it is made antithetical to science and can thus be blatantly attacked.

In fact, those who have gone through different kinds of political movements possess very strong analytical abilities. In the past, they had beliefs, disappointments, and blind worship, and they learned their lessons from these experiences. In particular, they endured an unforgettable blow to their souls during the Cultural Revolution. How can it be possible for these people to casually believe in anything? People today are the most capable of distinguishing clearly whether something is the truth or so-called "superstition" cooked up by political people.

Whether something is science or superstition is not to be decided by people involved in politics. Instead, it should be appraised by scientists. Yet the so-called "scientists" being used by political purposes are actually political figures as well. It is impossible for these kinds of people to genuinely draw a fair and scientific conclusion from an objective, scientific standpoint. This being the case, they cannot be called scientists whatsoever. At most, they can only serve as a club held in the hands of politicians and be used to strike at people.

The understanding of the truth of the cosmos by students of Dafa cultivation is their elevation through reason and application. It is futile for man, regardless of what perspective he takes, to negate the Fa and principles of the universe that are beyond all theories of human society. Especially when the morality of human society is on the verge of total collapse, it is the mighty universe that has once again shown great compassion and given mankind this final chance. This is the hope that mankind should treasure and cherish above all. Out of selfish desires, however, man is undermining this last hope the universe has granted him, thereby incurring the wrath of heaven and earth. Nevertheless, ignorant people take various catastrophes as natural phenomena. The universe does not exist for mankind. Man is only one form of expression of the lives existing at the lowest level. If mankind has lost the standard for existence at this level of the universe, it can only be eliminated by the universe's history.

Mankind! Wake up! The vows of Gods throughout history are being fulfilled. Dafa is evaluating all lives. The path of life is under one's own feet. A single thought of his own will also decide his own future.

Treasure and cherish it. The Fa and the principles of the universe are right in front of you.

Li Hongzhi
July 13, 1999

List of Falun Dafa Books in English

Zhuan Falun
China Falun Gong
Falun Dafa—Essentials for Further Advancement
Falun Dafa Lectures in the United States

For more information on Falun Dafa books and materials, please visit The Universe Publishing Company's website at

    http://www.universepublishing.com

— — — — — — — — — — — — — — —

Free Instruction and Workshops Worldwide

Falun Dafa practitioners provide free instruction and workshops worldwide. Books in different languages are available on Internet for free download. For further information, please visit the following websites:

        http://www.falundafa.org (USA)
        http://www.falundafa.ca (Canada)
        http://www.falundafa.au (Australia)

or call toll free: **1-877-FALUN99 (North America)**

Falun Dafa Books and Tapes Order Form

TO: The Universe Publishing Company
            P. O. Box 2026, New York, NY 10013
            Tel: (212) 343-3056 Fax: (212) 343-9512
            WebSite: www.universepublishing.com

Name: E-mail (if any):
Telephone: Fax (if any):
Address:

Shipping Address (if different from above):

ISBN and Description	Unit Price	Qty	Total
1-58613-100-1 China Falun Gong	$12.95	___	____
1-58613-101-X Zhun Falun	$12.95	___	____
1-58613-102-8 Falun Dafa—Essentials for Further Advancement	$ 7.95	___	____
1-58613-403-5 Falun Dafa Exercise Instruction Video Tape	$12.00	___	____

    SubTotal: ____
    NY Sales Tax 8.25% (For NY Residents Only):   ____
    Shipping ($2 per item):   ____
    Grand Total: ____

Please make your check or money order payable to:
  The Universe Publishing Company
  P.O. Box 2026, New York, NY 10013